FUN WITH LEATHER

FUN WITH LEATHER

How to do Decorative Leatherwork of
all kinds and how to make useful and
decorative articles from leather

by

Joseph Leeming

Illustrated by Charles E. Pont

PHILADELPHIA
J. B. LIPPINCOTT COMPANY
NEW YORK

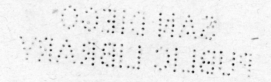

Designed by
CHARLES E. PONT

Printed in the United States of America

FOR
MADGE

FOREWORD

LEATHERCRAFT has been increasing rapidly in popularity during the past few years, and there are now thousands of enthusiastic devotees of this unique and fascinating type of craft work. There is good reason for this, for working with leather is a hobby that grows on one to a greater extent than most other comparable pursuits. Once the first few steps have been taken and one discovers how easy it is to transform a plain piece of leather into a beautifully finished handbag, book cover or picture frame, with finely-marked gold-leafed tooling or stamped designs, it is rare that anyone fails to become an ardent and permanent leather-craftsman.

Expensive equipment is not essential for leatherwork, nor is experience needed. There are many simple articles which even beginners at the craft can make without difficulty. When these have been made, more elaborate projects can be undertaken with confidence. At the same time, leatherwork affords a greater outlet for individual artistic and creative expression than many other crafts. Innumerable designs may be devised, striking coloring arrangements can be thought out, and new things to make or modifications of the articles described in the following pages can be developed.

There are only a few books available to the general reader in this country, which describe how to decorate leather and make leathercraft articles. The present volume has been prepared with the object of giving clear and simple directions, especially for those who have had no previous experience in working with leather, and also to provide instructions for making a greater number of leather articles than are available in other books dealing with the subject of leathercraft. It is the author's hope that the present volume will help many readers to discover the genuine pleasure that can be derived from working with leather—one of the most satisfying and interesting of all hobbies.

JOSEPH LEEMING

CONTENTS

PART I

PART II

MATERIALS, TOOLS, AND METHODS
PART I

MATERIALS, TOOLS, AND METHODS

HOW LEATHER ARTICLES ARE MADE

ATTRACTIVE, well-finished leather articles, such as portfolios, wallets, book covers, purses, desk sets, and a host of other things, are much easier to make than is commonly supposed. Care and patience are required in executing some phases of the work; but these qualities are needed for any type of craft work by means of which satisfyingly beautiful articles are created.

In the chapters that follow, each step involved in the making of leather articles is described in considerable detail. Right here at the outset, however, it will be helpful to outline the successive steps involved in transforming a piece of leather into a finished article such as, for example, the wallet which is used as an illustration.

The first step is to buy a piece of leather and a few tools. These can be purchased from any dealer in leathercraft supplies, of which there is one or more in every medium or large-sized city. If there is no supplier where you live, you will find advertisements of well-known and reliable dealers in such magazines as "Popular Mechanics" and "Popular Science Monthly."

The different kinds of leather, the purposes for which they are most suitable, and the sizes and shapes in which they may be purchased, are described in the chapter on "Kinds of Leather Used in Leatherwork." The tools that will be needed are described in the chapter on "Tools Used in Leatherwork."

Now, let us assume that you wish to make a wallet of the type illustrated in Fig. 1. The first thing you will need is a pattern. You can make your own pattern by studying and measuring a wallet of the type you wish to reproduce, or, for a few cents, you can buy a pattern from one of the dealers in leathercraft supplies. Patterns for a number of the most popular leather articles are given in this book, and the reader will be able to use them and will not have to obtain other patterns for a considerable period.

1

The pattern for the wallet is shown in Fig. 2. The pattern, in full size, is placed on the leather and a pencil is run around its edges to transfer its outline to the leather. The leather is then cut along the pencil lines with a sharp knife or a pair of shears. More detailed directions for cutting are given in the chapter on "Making the Pattern, Cutting and Skiving." (Skiving is the shaving or paring of the edges of a piece of leather so that when two pieces are laced together the joined edges will not be too thick or bulky.)

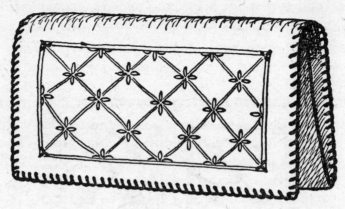

fig 1

The next step is to transfer to the leather the design that is to be used to decorate the finished article. The method by which this is done is described in the chapter on "Transferring the Design." The design for the wallet shown in Fig. 1, which consists of straight tooled lines and simple decorative figures, stamped on with a metal stamp, is shown in Fig. 2. Such designs are, of course, easy to originate and draw with the aid of a ruler. Other more elaborate designs are usually obtained from leathercraft supply dealers. They have available hundreds of design sheets from which the craftsman can select practically any type of design he may care to use. Geometrical patterns, foliated designs, ships, flowers, animals, decorative borders, medallions, monograms, and scores of other decorative figures are available.

Next comes the working up of the design by tooling, embossing, carving, or any one of the other processes for which instructions are given in the chapter on "The Different Kinds of Leatherwork."

With the wallet being used as an example, and with many other leather projects, it will be necessary to lace or thong certain parts together. How this is done is described in the chapter on "Lacing." In the case of the wallet, the lacing completes the work that has to be done to bring it to completion.

With some other articles, such as purses and handbags, snap fasteners are used. These are obtained from leathercraft supply dealers, who also have all the other needed accessories, such as key case frames with hooks to hold the keys, eyelets for belts, etc., buckles, leather tassels and buttons, and watch swivel snaps for lanyards designed to carry a watch or a whistle.

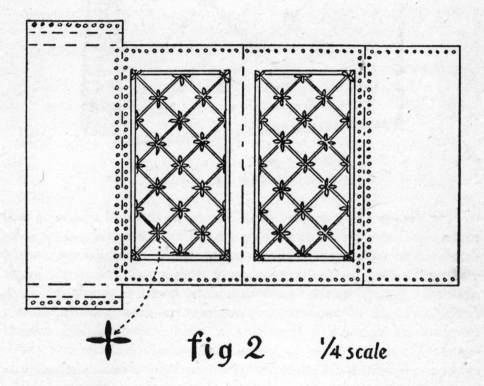

fig 2   ¼ scale

Many leather articles are dyed and others are waxed to give them a high polish after they have been completed. On other articles the design is gold-leafed or parts of the leather are colored by means of dyes or acids. Directions for doing these various types of work are given in the chapters that follow.

KINDS OF LEATHER USED IN LEATHERWORK

THE dealers in leather and leathercraft supplies are able to advise what kinds of leather are most suitable for making different articles, so that beginners do not need to be expert judges of the different kinds of leather. However, a working knowledge of the qualities of each important type of leather used in leatherwork is essential, and this information is given below.

A few general points should be noted. One is that chemical or chrome-tanned leathers cannot be tooled; only vegetable or bark-tanned leathers are suitable for this purpose. When selecting a skin, choose one that has a supple, even texture and is as free as possible from blemishes. The back is usually the best part of a skin and should be kept for important work, while the neck and sides may be used for small and less finely finished articles.

Some dealers sell leather in all sizes, but the majority offer it only in half hides (sides) or whole skins. Good tooling calf usually averages 10 to 14 square feet per skin and costs about 70 cents per square foot. Tooling calf shoulders, which are good for all ordinary tooling work, measure 3 to 4 square feet, and cost about 50 cents per square foot.

The most commonly used leathers are as follows:

Calf is suitable for nearly every kind of leatherwork. It is considered the best leather for tooling and modeling. It can be purchased in various colors and shades and in different thicknesses. It is very frequently used, uncolored, in its natural state. When tooled, the lines and areas worked over by the modeling tool acquire a rich dark brown color which contrasts beautifully with the lighter natural color of the unmodeled parts.

Cowhide is furnished with either a dull or a glossy finish. The dull type is specially prepared for staining. Cowhide can be tooled, modeled or carved, and is also used for hot-point or pyrographic work.

Oxhide is used for the same purposes as cowhide. It is usually a little stronger than cowhide, however, and so is particularly good for articles that will be subjected to hard wear.

Steerhide is strong and durable and is used for purses, billfolds, book covers, ladies bags, etc. It is a good tooling leather and comes in several colors—black, mottled brown, and russet. The russet color is especially suitable for dyeing.

Sheepskin is inexpensive and is therefore useful for beginners. It is rather loose in texture and stretches easily; but firm, even-grained pieces can be tooled if the work is done slowly and carefully.

Velvet sheepskin is an inexpensive suede or velvet finish leather, which comes in many colors. It is suitable for making leather pillows, book covers, moccasins, etc., and is excellent for pyrographic work.

Goatskin is very firm and tight-grained. It is the leather from which morocco leather is made, and this is used by expert leathercraftsmen for the finest grades of tooled and embossed work, as in bookbindings and finely ornamented boxes covered with morocco leather.

Pigskin is another tight-grained leather. It does not tool well, but is excellent for hot-point work, since the lines produced are a beautiful deep rich brown. It is used for wallets, billfolds, bags, bookbinding, and for other articles that will be subjected to hard wear.

Vellum or *parchment* is a thin, stiff leather which is produced either from sheepskins or calfskins, the latter type being the one usually preferred by leathercraftsmen. It can be decorated with water-color paints and is used for lamp shades, bookbindings, and illumination work.

Deerhide, elkskin and *horsehide* are sometimes used for leatherwork, particularly for making garments, moccasins, etc.

Crocodile, snakeskin, lizard, and *fishskin* are also occasionally used, sometimes to make bags, and sometimes to form decorations which are laced onto bags or other articles.

Skiver is a form of sheepskin split very thin. It is chiefly used as a lining material and for novelties such as rosettes, buttons, and tassels. When used as a lining, it is quite often glued or cemented to the article with which it is used.

TOOLS USED IN LEATHERWORK

THE tools needed for leatherwork can be purchased singly or in sets already made up by one of the many firms that sell leathercraft supplies. These tools are probably fewer in number and less expensive than those needed for any other type of craft work.

A good assortment of tools and equipments for the beginner would include the following

Leather cutting knife	Cutting board
Shears	Plate glass slab (about 12 by 12 inches)
Tracing tool	Leather punch
Modeling tool	Steel square
Stamping tool	Snap fastening setting outfit
Wooden mallet	

All these tools and pieces of equipment are shown in Fig. 3. Their uses are described below.

Leather cutting knife. A sharp-edged knife is required for cutting leather. Special knives for this purpose, with either a slanting or a square point, can be purchased for twenty-five cents. More elaborate knives, consisting of a wooden handle and several removable blades, can also be purchased. Many leathercraftsmen find that a razor blade fitted into a convenient handle is as satisfactory as a knife for general cutting purposes.

A leather cutting knife should be kept sharp at all times, and for this reason a leather strop or a sharpening stone should be kept at hand. Sharpening stones can be obtained at any hardware store, while leather strops mounted on convenient wooden handles can be purchased from leathercraft supply houses.

Shears are very useful as an adjunct to the cutting knife, being especially helpful for trimming rough edges and for cutting curved pieces of leather. Ordinary shears can be used; but a pair of florist's shears or tin snips are preferred by many craftsmen.

Tracing tool. This tool is used to trace on leather designs that have previously been drawn on a piece of paper. Such a tool can be purchased for about thirty-five cents. A perfectly adequate substitute for a regular tracing tool is an orangewood stick; and a large darning needle may also be used.

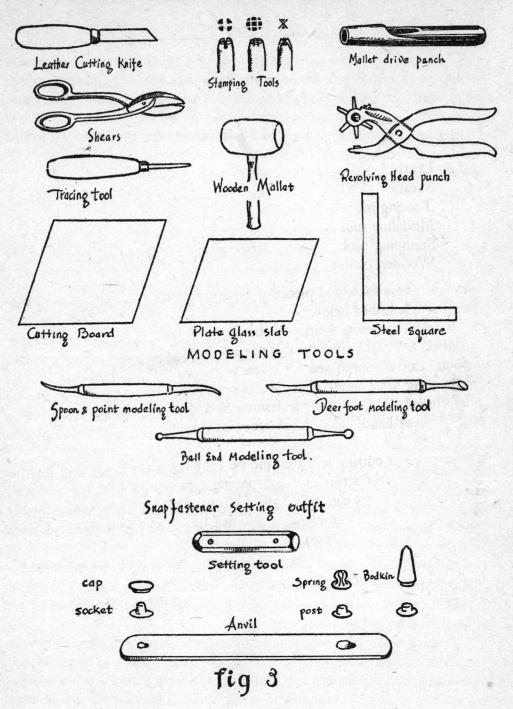

Leather Cutting Knife

Stamping Tools

Mallet drive punch

Shears

Wooden Mallet

Revolving Head punch

Tracing tool

Cutting Board

Plate glass slab

Steel Square

MODELING TOOLS

Spoon & point modeling tool

Deer foot modeling tool

Ball End Modeling tool.

Snap fastener setting outfit

Setting tool

cap

socket

Spring

Bodkin

post

Anvil

fig 3

Modeling tools. These tools are used for pressing down the background leather around the edges of a design which is to be tooled into relief. They come in various sizes and with differently shaped ends. Three types are shown in Fig. 3, a "spoon and point" tool, a "deer-foot" tool, and a "ball-end" tool. The ends on the tools most commonly used are usually shaped somewhat like spatulas and are slightly bent to allow the tool to rest on the leather while it is being pressed down. Ball-end modelers are generally used to model parts of a design into higher relief, as in embossing. This is done from the under side of the leather.

Stamping tools. These are used for stamping small decorative designs or figures on leather. An almost unlimited variety of decorations is made possible by using tools singly or in combination. Stamping tools usually cost about thirty-five cents each. A stamping tool to make small indented circles in the leather can be made by filing off the point of a medium-sized nail. Such a tool is often used to decorate the leather immediately surrounding the outlines of a design that has been brought into relief by tooling (see Fig. 9).

Wooden mallet. A wooden mallet is needed and will cost about fifty cents. It is used for striking the upper end of a stamping tool in order to impress the design on the bottom of the tool on the leather. The mallet is also useful for flattening seams and making creases.

Cutting board. Cutting boards are of two kinds—soft wood and hardwood. The soft wood board is used when leather patterns are being cut out with a knife or when parts of a design are being cut out in doing "cut-out" work. The soft grain permits the knife blade to penetrate slightly, thus cutting the leather clean and without turning or dulling the knife edge. Soft wood boards may also be used as a base upon which to place the leather when punching holes in it with a mallet drive punch. To keep the board in good condition, one side should be used exclusively for cutting and the other for punching.

Hardwood boards are likewise used for cutting and for punching holes in leather, and as a base upon which to place the leather when it is being tooled or stamped.

Some workers use a marble or plate glass slab as a base for cutting and tooling, and the marble slab is also used as a base for stamping work.

Leather punches. A punch is needed to make holes for the lacing which is used to finish off the edges of many articles made of leather, and to bind together the different parts of some articles, such as handbags, billfolds, etc.

Mallet drive punches, which are struck with the mallet, are available in eight sizes, each punch making a different sized circular hole. They vary in price according to size, the cost usually ranging from ten to fifty cents. To make a hole with such a punch, it is placed against the leather and is struck with a mallet.

Revolving-head punches are more convenient than the single-size mallet drive type of punch, for in a single tool they provide the means of punching four, six or eight different-sized holes. The usual cost of a revolving-head punch is from eighty cents to one dollar.

Steel square. Most leatherworkers use a steel carpenter's square for measuring leather and to serve as a guide when cutting straight edges. A square with a long arm measuring 12 inches and a short arm measuring 6 inches usually costs about twenty-five cents.

Snap fastener setting outfit. Many leather articles, such as purses, handbags, and key cases, are fastened by means of snap fasteners, sometimes called press studs. These are usually set in place before the article is sewed or laced.

A snap fastener has four parts. The spring fits over the post and forms the bottom part of the fastener, while the cap fits over the socket or eyelet and forms the upper part which is snapped down onto the lower part to fasten in place a purse flap or other part of a leather article. These parts are illustrated in Fig. 3a.

A snap setting outfit consists of a setting tool, an anvil, and a bodkin or needle, all of which are shown in Fig. 3. A wooden mallet is also needed.

Fig. 3a shows how a snap fastener is attached to a piece of leather. To set the spring on the post, the procedure is as follows: (1) Perforate the leather with a punch to receive the post. (2) Insert the post in the hole (see drawing A), and place the post on the anvil, with the small metal tip at one end of the anvil in the center of the post. (3) Place the spring on top of the leather over the post; place the setting tool over the spring, and strike it lightly with the mallet.

To set the cap on the socket: (1) Place the bodkin on the socket (see drawing B), and press the leather down over the bodkin. (2) Remove the bodkin and place the socket on the anvil with the large tip of the anvil in the center of the socket. (3) Place the cap on the protruding top of the socket, cover it with the setting tool, and strike the tool with the mallet.

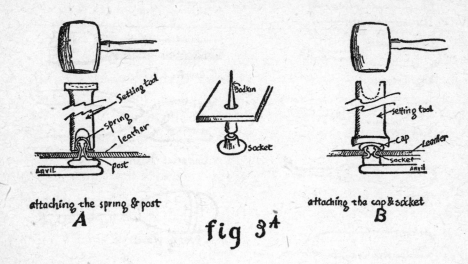

attaching the spring & post
A

fig 3ᴬ

attaching the cap & socket
B

The tools described above are ample for the beginner. Later on, after a few simple projects have been made and more difficult pieces of leatherwork are undertaken, other tools may be added from time to time as needed. Very few of these tools, however, will be needed by the amateur leather worker. They are illustrated in Fig. 4 and their uses are described below.

The *fid* or *belt awl* is used to enlarge punch holes, when necessary, to permit lacing to pass through readily. It is also used for stippling, tightening laces, etc.

The *edge creaser* is used for creasing the edges of belts and other articles, after trimming. There are two types, both shown in the drawing, one with a wooden handle fitted with a pronged metal creaser, and one made of a single piece of lignumvitae wood with creasing notches cut in each end.

The *edge trimmer* is used for rounding and smoothing the edges of leather articles to give them a finished appearance.

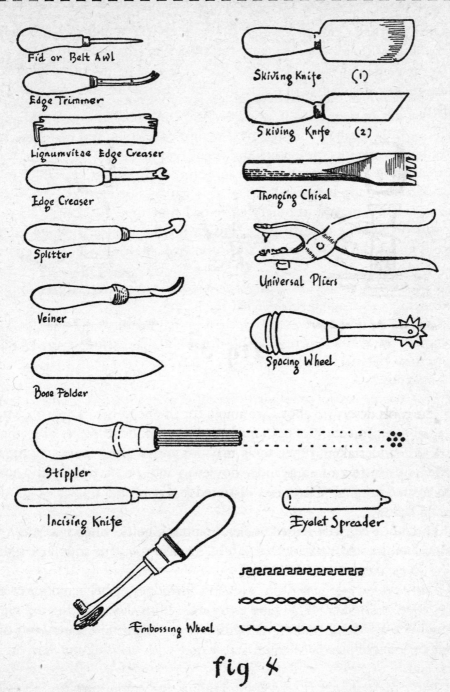

Fid or Belt Awl

Edge Trimmer

Lignumvitae Edge Creaser

Edge Creaser

Splitter

Veiner

Bone Folder

Stippler

Incising Knife

Embossing Wheel

Skiving Knife (1)

Skiving Knife (2)

Thonging Chisel

Universal Pliers

Spacing Wheel

Eyelet Spreader

fig 4

The *splitter*, which has a spade-shaped pointed head, is used to cut lines on heavy tooling leather.

The *veiner* is used for spreading lines cut with the splitter when preparing to tool thick leather.

A *bone folder*, so called because it is made of bone, is used for folding leather without scratching it, as might happen if a metal instrument were employed. It is handy for pressing down folded edges, and is also used to spread glue or cement smoothly and evenly on leather.

A *skiving knife* is used to thin or pare down leather, particularly at the edges. Skiving is especially needed when two or more thicknesses of leather are to be laced or otherwise joined together. By skiving or paring down the edge of each piece, unsightly thickness or bulging at the seam is avoided. Two types of knife are used, both of which are shown in Fig. 4.

The *thonging chisel* or *lacing awl*, usually with three prongs, is used for making and spacing slits needed for lacing.

Universal pliers consist of a standard punch handle, with a number of interchangeable attachments suitable for punching different-sized holes, fixing snap fasteners in place, setting eyelets, cutting slits for lacing, and other purposes.

The *spacing wheel* or *pricking wheel* is used by many leather workers for marking the exact centers of a series of holes to be punched for lacing near the edge of a piece of leather.

A *stippler* is a good tool for stippling backgrounds, and makes such work progress more rapidly than when the point of a modeling tool is used, since a stippler impresses a number of dots on the leather each time it is applied.

An *embossing wheel* is very useful for making decorative border designs, a few of which are shown in Fig. 4. Many leather articles such as wallets, cigarette cases, and leather covered boxes, may be decorated entirely with border designs made with an embossing wheel, or with a combination of such a border and one or more stamped designs. The designs are very frequently gold-leafed; but the wheel can also be heated and the designs burned into the leather.

Incising knife. This is a special thick-bladed knife which has a slanted end to the blade to permit it to rest at the correct angle on the line that is being cut.

Eyelet spreader or *eyelet setting tool*. This tool is used for putting eyelets in belts or other articles and for fastening key case frames in place. The leather is punched where each eyelet is to go. The eyelet is then inserted through the hole (in the case of a key case frame, through the hole in the metal frame also), and the eyelet spreader is placed on top of the eyelet and struck with a wooden mallet. This spreads out the top of the eyelet and secures it in place.

MAKING THE PATTERN, CUTTING OUT, AND SKIVING

Making the Pattern

IT is usually necessary to make a full-sized pattern of the leather article you wish to make. This pattern should be drawn on a piece of stiff paper or bristolboard, which will lie flat on the leather while a pencil is drawn around its edges to transfer its outlines to the leather. If a wallet such as the one shown in Figs. 1 and 2 or some similar article is being made, it is advisable to test the pattern by folding it at the points where the leather will have to be folded to make sure that the dimensions are correct, and that the edges meet perfectly when the wallet is folded.

Care should be taken to allow enough space on the pattern for the folds. The amount to allow varies somewhat with different types of leather. For calfskin, allow about one-half inch extra; for medium-weight cowhide, allow from one-quarter inch to one-half inch extra. By folding the paper or cardboard pattern, you can easily determine how much extra space should be allowed.

When the pattern is ready, place the leather you are going to use on a cutting board, a glass slab, or a piece of heavy cardboard, put the pattern on top of it, and fasten it down with thumb tacks around the edge or with weights. A sharp pencil, awl or bone folder may be used to mark round the edges of the pattern. It is best to mark the straight edges with the edge of a ruler or a steel straight edge.

Cutting Out

Remove the pattern from the leather when the marking has been completed, and cut along the outlines, using a knife and ruler or straight edge when cutting along straight lines, and scissors or shears for cutting curves. When using a cutting knife, always draw it toward you. Put the point of the knife in the line to be cut, push the ruler firmly against it, bear down on the ruler with the fingers of the left hand, and draw the knife toward you, cutting cleanly through the leather. A line should never be cut in two strokes, as this is apt to leave a rough edge.

Skiving or Paring

When the leather has been cut out, as described above, it is frequently necessary to skive or pare edges that are to be laced to other pieces of leather. This is to reduce the thickness of the leather so that the two edges joined by lacing will not bulge. Skiving is not needed if thin leather is being used, but is required for all medium-heavy and heavy leathers.

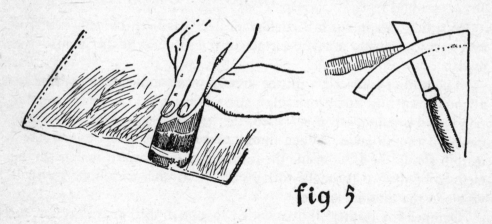

fig 5

A knife commonly used for skiving is one with a broad blade sharpened across the end. (See Fig. 4.) The sharpened part is beveled. The leather is placed on a glass slab or other smooth hard surface, and is held down firmly with the left hand. The knife is held in the right hand, with the beveled side of the blade on top. The thumb should be beneath the handle and the fingers on top of the blade, which is pushed away from the worker toward the edge of the leather. (See Fig. 5.)

Another type of skiving knife (see Fig. 4) is sharpened along one edge of the blade, as in a regular knife. With such a knife, the leather is pared along each edge, the blade moving from left to right, instead of away from the worker. Start skiving about two inches from one corner of the leather and move the knife to the corner. The knife point should be on the glass slab as the knife is moved along. Do not complete the skiving with a single cut. Skive off a thin layer with each cut until the leather is reduced to the desired thickness. (See Fig. 5.)

When the corner is reached, move the knife to a point about two inches to the left of the previous starting point and skive to that point. Continue in the same way until the skiving is completed.

The skiving should extend in about one-half inch from the edge of the leather. The edge should be skived to about one-half of its original thickness.

TRANSFERRING DESIGNS TO LEATHER

WHEN a design for a particular project has been chosen, it will be necessary to transfer it to the surface of the piece of leather that is to be used.

The leather is placed, with the dressed or smooth side uppermost, on a wooden cutting board or a glass slab. Some workers prefer the cutting board because, when it is used, the leather can be fastened to it by means of thumb tacks. When thumb tacks are used for this purpose, a margin should be left outside the outlines of the pattern for the thumb tacks to be pushed through. Otherwise, the thumb tack holes might be visible in the finished article.

Dampen the leather all over with a sponge dipped in cold water, and fasten the design paper to the leather with thumb tacks or with paper clips clipped over the edges of the leather and the design paper.

Then, with a tracing tool, an orange stick, or a hard pencil, go over all the lines of the design. Use a firm, steady pressure, so that you will not have to go over the same line twice, as this is apt to make a double line which cannot be removed. Once a line is transferred to the damp leather, it will stay there permanently.

It is a good idea to lift one edge of the design paper from time to time to make sure that the lines are being clearly impressed on the leather. If the design is a large one or takes a considerable length of time to trace, it may be necessary to dampen the surface of the leather again. If the transferred lines look like scratches, it means that the leather is too dry and should be dampened again.

Before removing the design paper, lift up and examine the design on the leather to make certain that all the lines have been transferred. If all the lines are on the leather, the design paper can be removed. Any lines that are not clearly defined can be gone over right on the leather with any tracing implement except a pencil. Pencils should never be used directly on the leather.

If a margin was left on the leather to take thumb tacks, it should now be trimmed off. You will then have the leather for the article you are making cut out to the right shape and size and imprinted with the design. The next step is to bring out the design by means of tooling, embossing, hot-point work, or one of the other methods described in the following chapter.

THE DIFFERENT KINDS OF LEATHERWORK

WHILE the most commonly used methods of decorating leather are probably tooling and stamping, there are a number of other processes which are frequently employed. Some, such as embossing and carving, are elaborations of ordinary tooling; while others, such as stenciling, mosaic work, and hot-point or pyrographic work, represent entirely different methods of decoration. The effects obtained by all the usual processes, and the methods of carrying them out, are described in this chapter.

Tooling or Flat Modeling

Tooling or flat modeling is the simplest and one of the most frequently used methods of decorating leather. It is accomplished by tracing a design on leather and then pressing down the background around the outlines of the design with a modeling tool, so the design stands out in low relief. (See Fig. 6.) Tooling also means to press down parts of the design so the background stands up in relief. An example of this may be seen in Fig. 1, where the straight lines are pressed down or tooled in this way. Frequently the background is stamped with a stamping tool making a plain circular mark or with a stippling tool. This serves to bring the design into greater emphasis.

Leathers recommended for tooling are bark-tanned calf, tooling cowhide and tooling steerhide. All leathercraft supply dealers sell "tooling" leathers, and one does not need to be an expert to select a suitable kind for the work intended, as the dealers will be able to recommend the right type for any project.

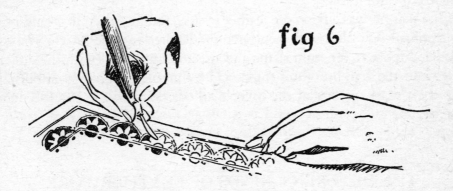

fig 6

When the design has been traced on the leather, the leather should be moistened again to prepare it for tooling. Another dampening may be necessary later on, as the leather should be kept moist throughout the period required for tooling. Care must be taken, however, not to soak the leather through so that water will be forced out by the pressure of the modeling tool. When too much water is used, the leather will not tool well and the water may cause the leather to curl and shrink. If you find that you have applied too much water, let the leather dry out and then moisten it again.

It is best to practice tooling a few times on some small pieces of leather before commencing to make a finished piece of leatherwork. A little practice will show you just how much to dampen the leather. Once the leather has been dampened, it should be handled carefully, since any scratches or other injury to the surface will not be removable.

When ready to do the actual tooling, place the leather on a glass or marble slab to ensure its lying flat. Then take a modeling tool and, putting its side against the design, press down the background leather immediately surrounding the design. Always move the tool away from the design. Frequently it is best to press the tool with a curving motion; at other points of the design a straight movement at right angles to the edge of the design will be better. After a little practice, no difficulty will be experienced in handling the tool in the most suitable manner.

When the tooling has been completed and the leather has dried, the parts that have been tooled or pressed down will be darker than the parts in relief, thus accentuating the design.

Embossing

Embossed leatherwork is also sometimes called leather repoussé or modeled leather. By embossing, the design is raised into high relief by modeling the back of the leather. The hollow spaces underneath the raised parts of the design are then filled in with a thick paste or other preparation to keep the raised portions in place. This type of work is widely used to decorate purses, bags, cushions, etc. (See Fig. 7.)

fig 7

Leathers commonly used for embossing are calfskin and cowhide. Sheepskin, a cheaper leather, can also be used and is good for beginners because of its low cost.

When doing embossing, the design must be transferred to both sides of the leather, with the lines on each side coinciding. There are several ways of accomplishing this. One is to trace the design in the usual way with a tracing tool on the smooth upper side of the leather. A piece of carbon paper is then placed underneath, with the carbon side next to the underside of the leather. Both leather and carbon paper are placed on the glass modeling slab, and the leather immediately surrounding the edges of the design is pressed down with a modeling tool. When this has been done, the outlines of the design will be defined on the underside of the leather by a blue line transferred from the carbon paper.

Some craftsmen employ the same method, but instead of carbon paper, use a piece of paper whose surface has been rubbed with white chalk. The paper is placed underneath the leather, with the chalked side uppermost, and the design is outlined in white on the underside of the leather.

Embossing may be done in either one of two ways: (1) with the leather turned over so the smooth or finished side is underneath, or (2) with the smooth side uppermost. The first way is probably the one most commonly used, but many experienced craftsmen prefer the second method. Each individual must experiment a little and find out which method is the easier for him.

When the first method is used, the leather is first turned over and dampened on the rough side. Its smooth, undampened side is then placed against a piece of rather thick felt, a piece of sponge rubber, a piece of corrugated cardboard, or against the palm of the left hand. The parts of the design to be raised are then pressed down with a modeling tool. Some workers prefer a ball-ended tool for this work, but it is by no means necessary, as embossing can be done perfectly with an ordinary modeler.

The leather is now turned over and placed on glass or on a hardwood board. The smooth surface, which is now uppermost, is dampened and the parts of the leather surrounding the raised design are pressed down with a modeling tool. It is always advisable to do embossing work slowly, so as to stretch the leather gradually. Some craftsmen prefer to work the underside until the design is partially raised, then work the smooth side, and then work again on the underside to complete bringing the design into the desired relief.

When embossing by the second method noted above, the leather is placed, with the smooth side uppermost, on a modeling board or table. Separate the thumb and forefinger of the left hand, and place the left hand on the leather so that the part of the design to be embossed is between the thumb and forefinger. (Some workers prefer to have the design between the first and second fingers of the left hand.) Take the modeling tool in the right hand and place it beneath the leather, with the point upwards. Then commence working it against the parts of the design that are to be raised.

Care should always be taken not to over-model or raise the design into too high relief. This produces an exaggerated, bumpy design which is not altogether pleasing.

When the embossing has been completed, the back of the raised design may be filled. The filling must be kept within the lines outlining the design on the underside of the leather. If it spreads over the lines, the finished work will not lie flat.

Thick paste and wax are used as filling materials, and tissue paper and rubber cement are also recommended. The tissue paper is placed flat, in layers, in the raised parts of the design, enough layers being used to fill the hollow parts. The paper is then coated with rubber cement.

When the filling is completed, the underside of the leather should be covered with thin muslin lightly glued in place. This may be covered with a piece of heavy silk or other decorative material.

fig 8

Stamping

Stamping is one of the simplest ways of decorating leather. It is done by means of metal stamps, each of which has a different design on one end. (See Fig. 8.) Stamping is sometimes called tooling, but it is more accurate to class flat modeling work only as tooling.

In stamping, the leather is dampened as for tooling, and is placed on a piece of soft wood or heavy cardboard. The stamping tool is then held upright on the points to be stamped, and is lightly tapped with a wooden mallet. If the top of the tool is struck too hard, the lower end may puncture the leather.

On some articles, designs may be stamped only in the four corners, while on others the entire background may be stamped in. The stamped parts may be left natural color, or be gold-leafed or painted to contrast with the leather.

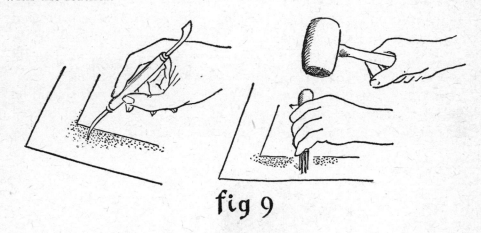

fig 9

Stippling

Stippling consists of making a number of small dots on leather, either with a special stippling tool or with the pointed end of a modeling tool. It is used chiefly for decorating some or all of the background of a design. It is done by simply marking the moistened leather with the end of the tool used (see Fig. 9), by hand if a modeling tool is used, or by a wooden mallet if a stippling tool is used.

Blind Tooling

In blind tooling the design is transferred to the leather by the usual method, but the tracing paper is left in place and is fastened to the leather by means of paper clips. Stamping tools with the designs that are to be impressed on the leather are then placed on the proper parts of the design on the tracing paper and are tapped lightly with a wooden mallet. When the stamping has been finished, the tracing paper is removed and the stamping tools are again applied to deepen the designs. Usually, each impression made by blind tooling is gold-leafed. This process is known as blind tooling because the design is stamped through the tracing paper. The method is the same as that used for stamping, which is illustrated in Fig. 8.

Cut or Incised Leatherwork

In this work the design is cut or incised with a special thick-bladed knife, the end of which is slanted so that it will rest at the proper angle on the cutting line. (See Fig. 4.) The incised lines are opened up with a tracing tool, and one side is pressed back into the background with a modeling tool. This is one of the most beautiful kinds of leatherwork, an example of which is shown in Fig. 10. It is sometimes called carved leatherwork.

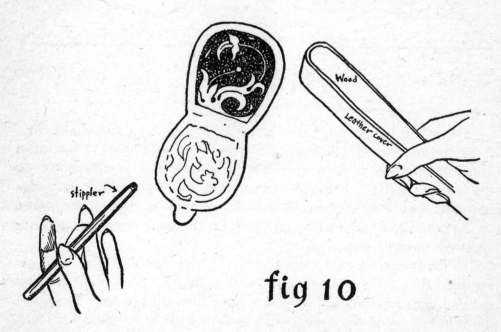

fig 10

Thick calfskin or cowhide should be used for incised leatherwork, and the special knife with a slant-ended blade. The leather is moistened as for tooling, and the design is transferred as already described. The tracing must be done very carefully, since a line that is wrongly incised cannot be altered.

For incising, the leather must be placed, smooth side upward, on a hard surface, preferably glass or marble. The leather should be dampened, but not too much, for if it is too moist it will stretch when being cut, and the lines will not be clean cut.

To cut straight lines, hold the knife so that the blade is at right angles to the leather, with the slanted edge parallel with the surface (see Fig. 11). Then draw the knife along the line to be incised, cutting through two-thirds of the thickness of the leather.

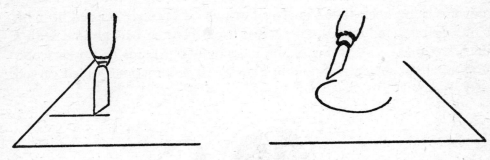

fig 11

When cutting curves, keep the blade at right angles to the leather, as before, but raise it a little more to the point (see Fig. 11). It is most important that the blade of the knife be always kept at right angles to the leather's surface. If the blade slants either to right or left, one edge of the cut will be soft, and no amount of tooling later on can make it firm.

At corners and where lines intersect, lift the knife out and commence again on the new line.

When the incising has been completed, the lines that have been cut are opened up with a tracing tool. This is done by placing the point of the tool in the incision and moving it once forward and once backward. Then press down the background leather with a flat modeling tool. Work up to the edge of the design and press down heavily on the edge of the cut away from the design so that it will be smoothed down into the background. While doing this part of the work, the leather must be kept damp or else the cut edge may rise later on. Another effective way to depress the background is to hammer it down with a stippling tool or a stamping which makes a number of small dots close together.

After the leather has dried, it should be waxed and polished.

Cut-Out Leatherwork

In this type of leatherwork the design is either traced or stenciled on the leather and certain portions of the design are cut out with a knife. The leather is then mounted on a piece of silk or leather of another color, which shows through the open spaces in the design. Cut-out leatherwork is used for cushions, table mats, lampshades, and similar articles. (See Fig. 12.)

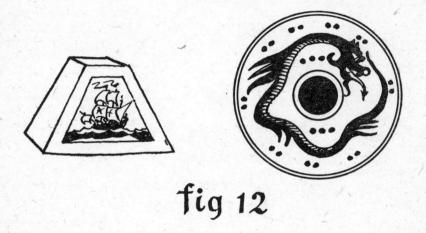

fig 12

Lamb and sheepskin are generally used for cut-out work, also thin calfskin. The work should be done on a soft wood cutting board and a sharp knife should be used, that cuts right through the leather, since if the leather pulls during the cutting, the design will be distorted. It is advisable to fasten the leather to the cutting board with thumb tacks. When cutting out the various parts of the design, hold the knife almost upright and cut each piece out cleanly, using considerable downward pressure on the knife.

When the design has been cut out, turn the leather over and apply cement or glue around the edges of the cut-out parts. Then lay the silk, leather, or other background material over the back of the leather, arranging it so its edges coincide with the outside edges of the leather. The leather should then be put under some books or other weights until the cement or glue has dried.

Leather Appliqué

In appliqué work, pieces of leather of various shapes or designs are cut out and are cemented or glued to another piece of leather. Flower shapes may be cut out and colored, for example, and then be used to decorate a table runner, table mat, leather cushion, or leather screen. (See Fig. 13.)

fig 13

Leather Inlay or Leather Mosaic

In this work the design is inlaid with small pieces of colored or contrasting leather, portions of the original leather being removed to make room for the inlaid pieces. It is work that requires skill and accuracy and should be practiced on small scraps of leather before undertaking a real project. (See Fig. 14.)

Calf, cowhide, and morocco grain goat are all good for background materials. Two methods are commonly used for inlay work, both of which are described below.

In the first method the design is marked on the surface of the leather, and a sharp knife is then run around the edges of the parts that are to be removed to make room for the inlaid pieces. The knife should cut about half way through the background leather. The parts to be removed are then cut away by horizontal under-cutting with the knife. Each piece that is removed is placed on the leather that is to be inlaid, and is used as a pattern for the cutting out of the piece that is to take its place. The inlay pieces are cut out by running a sharp knife around the edges of the patterns. When they have been cut out they are glued or cemented in place.

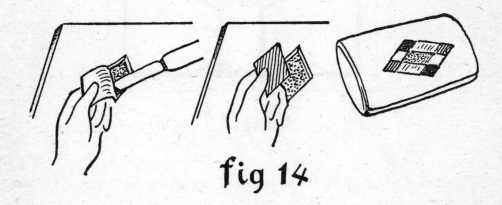

fig 14

In the second method, two different-colored pieces of leather of the same size and shape are lightly cemented together with rubber cement. The design is transferred to the top piece, both pieces are fastened to a cutting board with thumb tacks, and the parts that are to be inlaid are cut out with a knife held perpendicularly, which cuts through both pieces of leather at the same time.

The two pieces of leather are then separated, and the top piece is cemented to a thin leather base of the same size and shape. The pieces cut from the bottom piece of leather are fitted into the holes in the top piece. They are held in place by cement, which is applied before they are inlaid.

In the same way, the pieces cut from the top piece of leather may be inlaid in the holes that were cut in the bottom piece, making a second piece of inlay work.

Stenciled Leather

Many leather articles can be beautifully decorated by stenciling colored designs on them. (See Fig. 15.) A stencil is a thin sheet of cardboard in which spaces are cut to make a design. In transferring the design to a piece of leather, the leather should be placed on a table or other flat surface. The stencil is then placed on the surface of the leather and is held down by the fingers of the left hand. The coloring material is

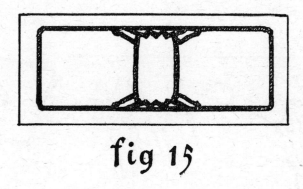

fig 15

applied to the leather by drawing a brush across the open spaces, forming the design, that are cut in the stencil. Stencils already cut out can be obtained from Leathercraft supply dealers, or the stencils may be made at home. For home-made ones, almost any stout cardboard may be used, but there is a special stencil board which is treated to prevent paint from penetrating from side to side. This kind can be obtained at art supply stores and is recommended, since it ensures that no paint will work through and color the leather outside the edges of the design. The spaces that compose the design should be outlined on the cardboard with a pencil, and should then be cut out with the sharp point of a pen-knife blade.

This method of decoration is suitable for table mats and runners, cushions, bookmarks, purses made of suede or chamois, magazine covers, and other similar articles. Suede, velvet calf, and sheepskin are frequently used as a background for stenciled designs. Leather enamel, water colors, leather dyes, and artists' oil paints mixed very thin with turpentine, may all be used for coloring. Use a soft stencil brush and apply only a little color at first. When the first application has dried, other coats may be added if deeper tones are desired.

Hot-Point or Pyrographic Work

This method of decorating leather is similar to the method used for decorating wood by pyrography or burning in the outlines and shading of figures and designs. Pigskin is generally used for the work, but other kinds of tight-grained leather are also suitable, also suede leather.

The burning is done by means of a pointed tool such as a modeling tool, which is heated in a sootless flame. The tool must be hot enough to brown the surface of the leather, but should not be over-heated so that it burns the leather. A few experiments on leather scraps will show how hot the point should be. Care must be taken not to burn too deeply, as there is a possibility of burning a hole through the leather.

Hot-point work, as mentioned above, can be used to outline designs

fig 16

and to shade them. (See Fig. 16.) It is also used when painting on suede leather, since in this case it is needed to keep the colors from running and mixing with each other.

Leather Patchwork

Many colorful and attractive articles can be made from leather scraps left over from other work. Stained and dyed leathers of contrasting colors should be chiefly used. Patchwork is mostly used as a decoration and can be employed effectively on leather cushions, bags, purses, desk blotter pads, moccasins, etc. (See Fig. 17.)

The first step is to draw a pattern of a patchwork design on a piece of paper. Then cut out different-colored pieces of leather and fasten each one in its place on the pattern with rubber cement. Put the work under books or other weights until the cement has dried. The work is then cemented to the leather which it is to decorate. On the other hand, the pieces may be separated and then laced together in a large piece of work such as a pillow cover.

fig 17

LACING OR THONGING

THE most commonly used method of joining together edges of leather articles is by means of leather lacing, also called thonging. This is not only stronger than machine stitching, but is also more decorative and adds to the beauty of the article being made. In addition to its use for joining edges, lacing is also used to fasten appliqué decorative figures onto a leather background.

Leather lacing can be purchased from all dealers in leathercraft materials. The price is usually five or six cents a yard, and it is furnished in widths ranging from 1/16-inch to 1/4-inch. The width most commonly used is probably 1/8-inch.

Some workers prefer to cut their own lacing. Long strips can be cut from a piece of leather by placing it on a cutting board and using a straight edge and a sharp knife. The leather should be thin calf, goat or cowhide. Another way of cutting lacings is to cut out an oval or circular

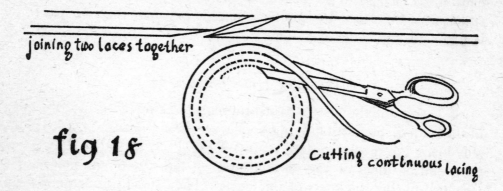

joining two laces together

fig 18

Cutting continuous lacing

piece of leather and then cut around its edge with a pair of shears. (See Fig. 18.) This produces a long strip. After it is cut, the lacing should be straightened by wetting it thoroughly and pulling it several times between the left thumb and forefinger. It is best to hold a piece of folded leather between the thumb and forefinger when this is being done.

Joining Two Laces Together

It may sometimes be necessary to join a new piece of lacing onto the end of the piece you have been working with in order to continue the work. To do this, skive the two ends diagonally, one from the top and the other from the bottom (Fig. 18). Cover the diagonal surfaces with cement or glue and press them together. Use a spring paper fastener or a spring clothespin to hold the two ends together until the cement or glue has hardened.

Preparing Edges To Be Laced

The two edges that are to be laced together should be skived or pared down on the flesh or unfinished sides to one-half their original thickness.

Some workers like to fasten the edges together, after they have been skived, with rubber cement or glue. This holds the edges together during the lacing. Others prefer not to use a cement as it may make the edge of the work rather stiff. If cement is used, it should be applied sparingly and should not be applied within an inch of the points at which the lacing is to start and end. These spaces must remain open so that the ends of the lacing can be tucked in. When the lacing is completed, the spaces may be closed by applying cement between the two pieces of leather with the blade of a knife.

Punching Holes For Lacing

In lacing, the thongs are passed through holes punched near the edge of the leather. Several kinds of punches are used, the most popular probably being the revolving-head type (see Fig. 3), with either four, six or eight cutting tubes of varying dimensions. The size of the holes is determined by the thickness of the lacing. They should be large enough for the lacing to pass through without tearing or pulling, but not so large as to leave a space around the thongs.

Straight holes or slits are preferred by some workers and these are made with a pronged thonging chisel or lacing awl of the type shown in Fig. 4.

The holes are usually placed at a distance of from ⅛-inch to ⅜-inch in from the edge, the distance depending upon the thickness of the leather and the size of the article.

When marking the points at which the holes are to be punched, it is a good idea first to mark the place where a hole is to go in the middle of a corner. Then mark for a hole on each side of this point and rather close to it. The remaining space may then be marked for holes equidistant from each other, the space between the holes being approximately the same length as the distance that the holes are in from the edge of the leather.

To ensure accurate spacing, which is necessary for good work, a space marker or pricking wheel may be used. (See Fig. 4.) This is not essential, however, as many workers use a ruler to measure the spaces and mark the places for the holes with an awl or the point of a tracing tool or modeling tool.

When the holes have been punched along the edge of one of the pieces of leather that is to be laced, lay the edge face down on the edge of the other piece of leather and mark through the holes to indicate the positions for the holes in the second piece.

Kind of Lacing

The most frequently used methods of lacing leather articles are illustrated in Fig. 19.

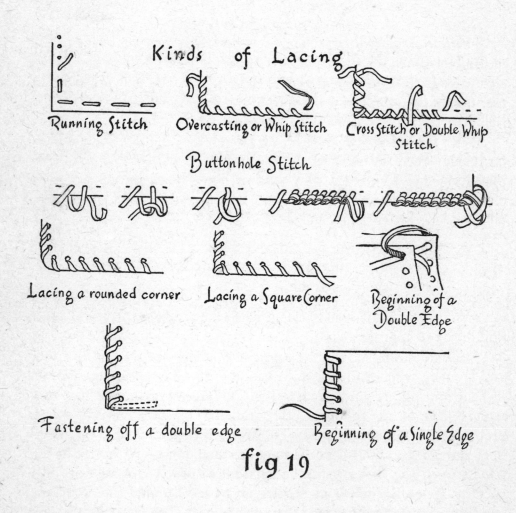

fig 19

The *Running Stitch* is the simplest method of lacing. It requires a lace about one-and-one-half times as long as the edge or edges that are to be joined.

The *Overcasting* or *Whip Stitch* requires a lace about three times as long as the edge to be laced. This is a very popular method of lacing and adds an attractive finish to the article being made.

The *Cross-Stitch* or *Double Whip Stitch* is done similarly to the Overcasting or Whip Stitch, but twice the length of lacing is required and both ends are used in working. When making each stitch, one end is pushed through a hole down from the top and the other end is then pushed up through the same hole from the bottom.

The *Buttonhole Stitch* is the most decorative of all the stitches. The method by which it is made is clearly shown in Fig. 19. It requires a lace about five times as long as the edges to be joined, and it is preferable to use straight holes or slits made with a thonging chisel, as these keep the lacing flatter.

When the lacing is completed, the two ends of the lace are concealed by tucking them in between the two pieces of leather that have been joined together. They are then fastened down by means of cement or glue. It is usually best to skive the ends to reduce their thickness, so they will not cause an unsightly bulge.

SEWING LEATHER

LEATHER may be sewed, either by hand or on a sewing machine, and this is sometimes preferable to lacing when the article is small or a sewed finish is more appropriate.

Small holes, marked out by a pricking wheel and punched with an awl, are used when leather is to be hand sewed. The three stitches used in hand sewing are illustrated in Fig. 20 and are so simple that they require little or no comment. The running stitch is the one that is probably most commonly used. The article is first stitched in one direction, and is then stitched in the opposite direction to fill up the spaces left between the first stitches. The saddler's stitch is done with two needles. At each stitch both needles are passed through the same hole, one from the top and the other from the bottom. The backstitch is done

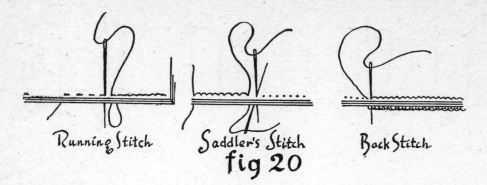

Running Stitch   Saddler's Stitch   Back Stitch
fig 20

with a single needle, the method followed being shown in the drawing.

Strong thread should be used for sewing, and it should be as nearly as possible the color of the leather. If the thread is waxed with beeswax, it will be firmer and less likely to twist or knot during the sewing.

When sewing leather on a sewing machine, a piece of paper should be placed between the leather and the feed of the machine to prevent marking or scarring. A long, loose stitch should be used, and the sewing should be done slowly. The last few stitches are secured to the leather by means of glue. This kind of sewing is generally used for sewing pockets to the lining of a handbag or billfold, and for other similar work.

GUSSETS

MANY handbags, brief cases, and other similar articles made of leather are fitted with gussets to make the pocket or interior more roomy. The principal types of gussets are illustrated in Fig. 21. Usually, gussets are made of the same leather as the main part of the article, but a thinner leather is sometimes used when there are several pockets or divisions which require more than one pair of gussets.

Gussets should be cut a little longer than the end space they are to fit. About ¼ of an inch extra should be allowed at the bottom, and ⅜ of an inch at the top. When punching a gusset for lacing, punch the top hole in each side first and tie the gusset into its proper position in the end of the bag or other article. (The lacing holes have already been punched in the main part.) Next punch a hole in the center of the bottom of the gusset to correspond with the hole that has already been

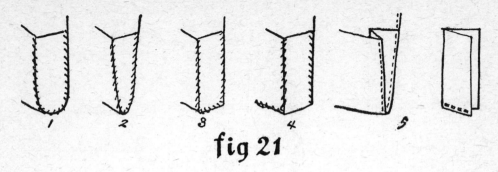

fig 21

punched in the main part of the article at this point, and tie a short piece of string or thread through the two holes.

Now hold the edges of the gusset and the main part evenly together and, with an awl, mark through the holes that have been punched in the main part. Untie the gusset and punch holes in it through the marks made by the awl.

Skive the extra ⅜ of an inch of leather at the top of the gusset, fold it down inside, and fasten it to the rest of the gusset with glue or cement. This makes a strong edge that will not tear.

Gussets Nos. 1, 2, and 3 are made in pairs, one gusset being inserted in each end of the bag or other article. No. 4 is a continuous gusset, made of a single piece of leather, which fills both ends and the bottom of the article. No. 5 is sometimes convenient to use and can be made either with the running stitch, as shown, or with an overhand stitch. It consists of a rectangular piece of leather which is folded and hammered down the center. At the lower edge, approximately ⅛ of an inch is cut from the folded edge, gradually sloping down to the outer corner. This part is joined together with two or three stitches of running lacing, the ends of the lace being secured with glue.

When lacing a continuous gusset, such as No. 4, there is a tendency for the article to become twisted. To prevent this, the lacing of the two edges should be worked in opposite directions. First lace one edge completely, and then start on the other edge at the end just completed and work back to the opposite end, so that the lacing stitches slant in opposite directions, as shown in the drawing.

POLISHING AND COLORING LEATHER

Polishing Undyed Leather

THE usual leathers used for tooling, such as calf and cowhide, should usually be polished to bring out their color and texture, if they are not going to be dyed or otherwise colored. A number of brands of solid wax polish suitable for this purpose are on the market and can be purchased at department or hardware stores. The wax should be applied with a woolen cloth or a sheepskin shoe polisher. Use only a small amount of wax and rub lightly so that the cloth or other polisher will not mark the surface of the leather.

Undyed leather may also be polished with shoe cream or banana oil. A very attractive effect can be obtained on natural color leather by going over its surface with a sponge that has been dipped in waterproof brown ink, and then waxing the leather after the ink has dried. When this is done, the ink soaks into the pores of the leather and brings out the natural beauty of the grain.

Polishing Dyed Leather

When leather has been dyed, it should be polished with a solid wax polish, as described above. The cut-out pieces should be waxed before they are assembled in order to protect the leather from stains, glue or finger marks. After the solid wax polish has dried, a coat of liquid polish may be applied.

Coloring Leather

The beauty of many articles made of leather is very considerably increased if parts of the design are colored. Leather may be colored either by means of dyes or acids, both methods being commonly used. When the leather is to be colored by means of dyes, it must first be thoroughly cleaned to free it from dirt or grease. If this is not done, it will not be possible to get the coloring evenly distributed on the surface of the leather. When coloring by means of acids, the leather need not be cleaned.

To clean a piece of leather, place it on a glass slab with the smooth or finished side uppermost, and dampen it evenly with a sponge or piece of cotton that has been dipped in cold water. Dip another sponge into a weak solution of oxalic or hydrochloric acid and rub it evenly and firmly over the surface of the leather. The acid will remove all grease or dirt.

Potassium and caustic soda are also used for cleaning leather. All dealers in leathercraft supplies carry these chemicals and provide complete directions concerning the strength of solution to be used, so beginners will have no difficulty in knowing just how to apply them.

Coloring Leather With Dyes

Dyes of all colors for coloring leather may be purchased from all dealers in leathercraft supplies. They come in both powdered and liquid form, and the latter kind is recommended to beginners as it is rather difficult to mix the powdered dyes.

Be sure to experiment at first by coloring scraps of leather, for dyeing requires a certain amount of practice and should not be tried on a piece of leatherwork that may have taken several hours to prepare and tool, unless the worker is confident of the results he will obtain.

The leather to be dyed should be placed on a board and dampened as for tooling. The dyes are then applied with a swab, usually furnished with the bottle, or, if large areas are to be colored, with a sponge or absorbent cotton. If the leather does not take the dye well, it should be sponged with a weak solution of ammonia—a few drops to a half glass of cold water.

When small parts of a design are to be colored, and when two or more colors are to be used, it is best to use a small camel's hair brush. It is also advisable to apply only a thin coat at first and add a second coat, if necessary, for light shades can always be deepened, but deep or dark tones cannot be lightened.

On some leathers dyes have a tendency to run. This may be prevented to a certain extent by adding a pinch of sugar to a tablespoonful of the dye.

Coloring Leather With Acids

Acids are frequently used to color leather and produce very lovely soft shades. They are usually purchased in crystal form and are added to cold water to make a saturate or near-saturate solution. Care must be taken not to make the solution too strong, since it might harm the leather. When you make a solution, always experiment with it on leather scraps to see if it is the correct or desired strength.

The following acids are the ones most commonly used:

Potassium is used for making practically all shades of brown, ranging from beige to chestnut. A weak solution made by adding six drops of the prepared mixture that is sold at drug stores to a half glass of water should be used. To obtain the darker shades, several applications should be made. If you wish to remove any coloring done by means of potassium, this can be done with hydrochloric acid while the leather is still wet.

Caustic soda may be used in the same manner as potassium. It is not quite so strong, and eight to ten drops should be mixed with a half glass of water.

Bichromate of potash gives varying shades of brown, and is sometimes used as a foundation for brown dyes or for giving an antique finish to natural leather. Mix seven or eight drops with a quarter of a glass of water.

Picric acid gives a pale yellow color. When applied over a coat of iron sulphate it gives a beautiful shade of soft green, varying in depth according to the strength of both acids. It is chiefly used as a foundation or in conjunction with other acids or dyes.

Sulphate of iron, in weak solution, gives varying shades of gray, ranging from dove-gray to deep blue-gray. When sulphate of iron is applied over potassium, a dead black results.

APPLYING GOLD LEAF

MANY tooled and stamped designs may be given an exceptionally attractive finish by gold-leafing them. Leather-covered boxes, calling-card cases, book covers, cigarette cases, and other similar articles are all suitable for this type of decoration. Calfskin, cowhide, and good sheepskin may be used for gold-leaf work. The design is traced on the leather in the usual way and the design is modeled, except the parts or figures that are to be made by stamping. Stamping, when it is to be gold-leafed, is always done after the leaf has been applied.

When the tooling is completed, the parts that are to be gold-leafed are given a coat of gold size. This is obtained from the dealer from whom the gold leaf is purchased. All bubbles in the size should be brushed out and the first coat allowed to dry thoroughly. A second coat may not be necessary, especially on calfskin. The leather should be bent where it has been coated, and if the bent part appears lighter than the rest, a second coat will be needed.

After the first or second coat, as the case may be, has dried, apply a very thin coat of size and let it dry until it becomes sticky or "tacky," which usually requires twenty to thirty minutes. Then take a sheet of the gold-leafed tissue from the book in which it is supplied, and put it on the sized part of the design, with the metal side down. Press the tissue into the design with the fingers. The gold leaf will adhere to the leather, and the tissue can be removed.

The gold leaf should be allowed to dry thoroughly, which usually takes about six hours. Any surplus metal is then brushed off with a piece of linen cloth or chamois leather. Designs to be made by stamping are then stamped in after the gold leaf has dried. All parts of the design that are not gold-leafed are usually given a finishing coat of white spirit varnish. Any gold adhering to the leather outside the edges of the parts to be gold-leafed can be removed by rubbing with a cloth moistened in turpentine.

THINGS TO MAKE OF LEATHER
PART II

CALLING CARD CASE

THE calling card case shown in Fig. 22 is made of suede leather and is laced with suede thongs. It is very easy to make, since it consists simply of two pieces of leather cut to the shape shown and laced together. Measurements are governed by the size of the calling cards which the case is intended to hold.

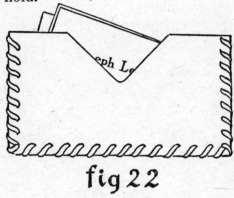

fig 22

A COMB CASE

THE comb case illustrated in Fig. 23 is very simple to make, since it consists only of two pieces of leather cut to the proper shape and laced

fig 23

together. Suede is a good type of leather to use for such a case and it can be laced with suede thongs. Tooling calf or cowhide or other forms of grained leather may, of course, also be used.

The size of the case will depend upon the size of the comb. To fit most pocket combs, the case will measure about 5 inches long and 1½ inches wide. The decoration can consist of the initial of the person for whom the case is being made, or of a monogram.

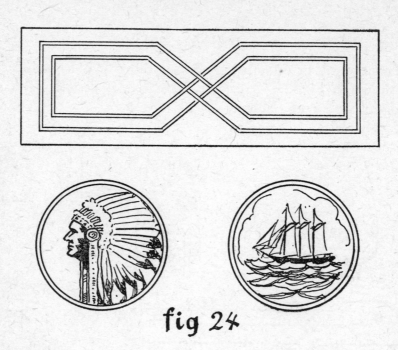

fig 24

TABLE MATS

DECORATIVE leather table mats are always welcome as gifts and are useful for a number of purposes. They can be made of tooling calf or sheepskin and decorated with a tooled or stamped design, or of suede, in which case the designs can be brought out by means of hot-point work or dyes. Stenciled designs are also frequently used on leather mats. Many mats are made of leather that is purchased already commercially dyed an attractive color. After tooling, contrasting dyes may be applied to different parts of the design.

Even for a simple square, rectangular or circular mat, it is best to make a paper or light cardboard pattern before cutting the leather. Place the pattern on the leather and trace around its edge as already described.

The leather is then dampened and the design is transferred to it. The principal lines of the design may then be tooled or emphasized by one of the other methods of leather decoration mentioned above.

A KEY CASE

TOOLING calf or any other good firm leather may be used for the key case shown in Fig. 25. It can be decorated, if desired, with a tooled monogram or a more elaborate design.

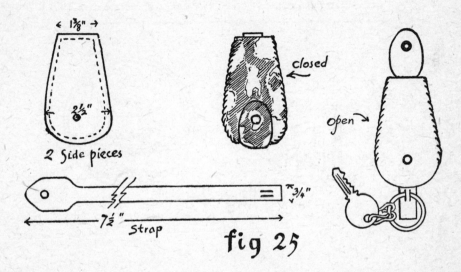

fig 25

The case is made from three pieces of leather. Two pieces, each the same size and shape, form the sides, and a strip of leather holds the key ring at one end and has a snap fastener on the opposite end. When the keys are inside the case, this strip extends along one side and around the bottom to the spring or stud of the fastener.

Cut a paper pattern for each piece and cut the pieces from the leather. The top part of a snap fastener should then be inserted in the broad end of the leather strip. Two slits are cut in the opposite end and a circular key ring fitted through them as shown. Next put several keys on the key ring and place the strip between the two sides of the case. Pull the keys inside the case, and pass the strip down one side of the case, around the bottom, and up the other side. Mark the point underneath the cap of the snap fastener and insert the spring of the fastener at that point.

The case is then completed by lacing the two sides together by means of a simple overcasting or whip stitch.

ANOTHER KEY CASE

THIS is another kind of key case—one that folds around the keys and fastens with a snap fastener. The piece marked A, in Fig. 26, measures

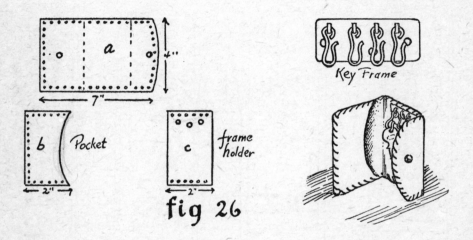

fig 26

7 inches long and 4 inches wide, and is made of tooling calf. The two smaller pieces, B and C, each measure 2 by 4 inches, and are made of calf lining leather. In addition you will need some leather lacing and a key case frame fitted with four or six swivel hooks. This can be obtained from a leathercraft supply dealer.

Cut out the three pieces, as shown, and punch the holes that are indicated. Next fasten the key frame to piece C by means of the eyelets furnished with the frame and an eyelet spreader.

Now assemble the pieces. The piece with the key frame, C, is placed in the center of the large piece of leather and is cemented to it. The other small piece, B, forms a pocket on the left side of the large piece, A. It is held in place by means of lacing, which is continued all the way around the case.

If you wish to have a design, some initials or a monogram, on the outside of the case, it should be tooled in before the pieces are assembled. Instead of making the pocket with the small piece of leather, B, you can use celluloid or some other transparent material so that the case can be used to carry an automobile license or identification card. Strips of transparent material for this purpose can be purchased from any leather-work supply dealer.

BOOKMARKS

BOOKMARKS, such as those shown in Fig. 27, are among the easiest of

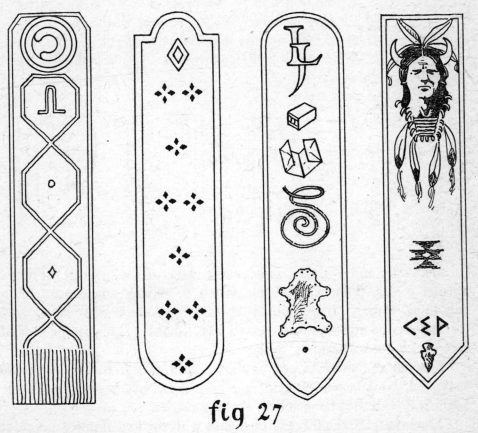

fig 27

all leather articles to make. They consist simply of pieces of leather about 6 inches long and from 1 to 1½ inches wide, which may be rectangular or pointed. A decorative figure or a monogram may be placed near the top. This may be a simple tooled design, a stamped figure, or a design finished by means of hot-point work or dyeing with bright colors. The balance of the bookmark may be left plain or may be decorated by stamped designs made by using one or more stamping tools. A finished appearance is given to the completed bookmark by beading or creasing the edges with an edge creaser.

TOBACCO POUCH

TOBACCO pouches of the convenient design shown in Fig. 28 may be made of suede, pigskin, calfskin or cowhide. They are both attractive and useful, and are easy to make. Two pieces of leather are used, one for the back of the pouch and the flap, the other for the front. When the pieces have been cut out and laced together, a rubber lining may be cemented on the inside.

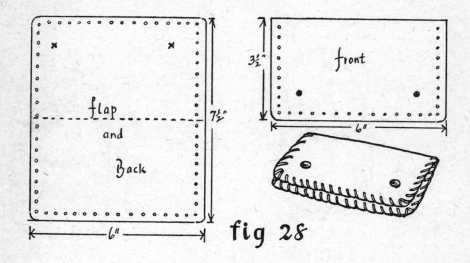

fig 28

A COIN PURSE

THE triangular coin purse shown in Fig. 29 is made of calf tooling leather. Cut a paper pattern similar to the one shown in the drawing, and fold it along the dotted lines to make certain that the different sections are the right shape and that their edges coincide exactly when the pattern is folded into the shape of the completed purse.

Cut out the leather and fasten the two parts of a snap fastener to it, as indicated in the drawing. Then, if the purse is to be decorated, dampen the leather and model the design. Fold the leather to form the purse and either lace or stitch the two side edges together. To complete the purse, crease the edges with an edge creaser.

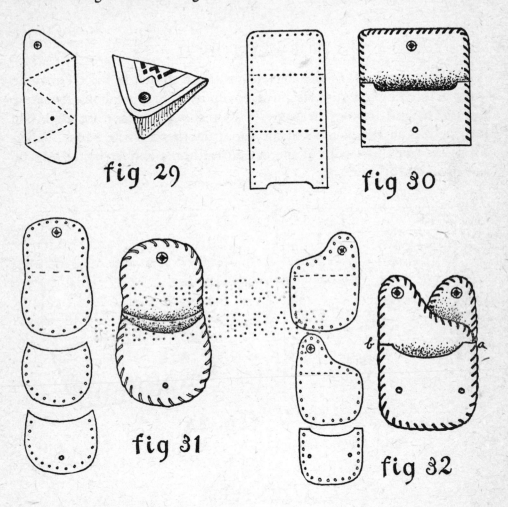

fig 29   fig 30

fig 31   fig 32

COIN PURSE

Fig. 30 shows a rectangular coin purse. It is made from a single piece of calf tooling leather of convenient size, which is folded over twice to form a pocket and a flap. A simple design, initials, or a monogram may be tooled on the outside of the flap. The sides may either be stitched or laced. If lacing is used, start at the right-hand lower corner and work right around the edge to the lower left-hand corner.

COIN PURSE

FIG. 31 shows a convenient two-compartment purse, which is made of three pieces of calf tooling leather. Cut a paper pattern for each piece, and fit the pieces together to be sure that the edges coincide. Then cut out the leather pieces and set the two parts of the snap fastener in position. Complete the purse by lacing or else stitching the three parts together. If lacing is used, start lacing on the left-hand side at the point where all three pieces of leather come together, and continue all the way around the edge.

COIN PURSE

THE coin purse shown in Fig. 32 has two compartments and two flaps, and is made of three pieces of calf tooling leather joined together by lacing or stitching. The outer flap should be slightly larger than the inner one, in order to appear even when the purse is closed. If lacing is used, start at *a* and work around the outer flap; then around the inner flap. This will bring you back to *a*, from where the lacing is continued on around the bottom of the purse to *b*.

PURSE WITH A TUCK-IN FLAP

THIS convenient little purse is made from a single piece of leather, which is cut to the shape shown in the drawing. Suede is suggested as a good leather to use, and the lacing should also be of suede. Fold the bottom of the leather upward to form the pocket, and then fold the pointed top down in order to determine the correct place to cut the slit which holds the tuck-in flap. Then punch for lacing and lace along the two sides, and also across the top of the pocket. (See Fig. 33.)

If you wish, you may line the purse with lining leather, so that the tip of the flap will not protrude into the interior of the purse. If this is done, the lining leather should be cut to the same size and shape as the outside piece, and should be laced to the outside piece along the two sides and the top.

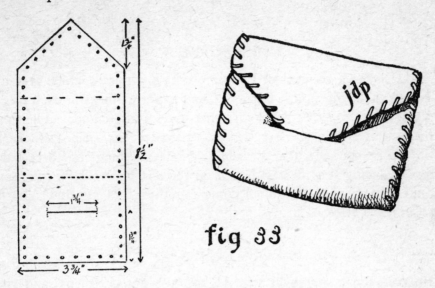

fig 33

PHOTOGRAPH ALBUM OR SCRAP BOOK COVER

COVERS for photograph albums, scrap books or autograph books are easy to make, since they consist only of two pieces of leather, one for the front and one for the back.

The leather used should be fairly heavy tooling calf or cowhide. The dimensions will depend, of course, upon the page size of the book or album. The front cover may be decorated by means of a medallion or a more elaborate "all-over" design, or may have a single or double line tooled around the edges. Another idea is to tool a word, such as *Photographs*, *Snapshots*, or *Autographs* on the cover.

When the design has been completed, punch two holes ½-inch in from the left-hand edge of each piece of leather to take the lacing by which the pages of the book and the covers are held together. If ready-punched pages are purchased for the book, the holes in the cover pieces should correspond with the holes in the paper. If you are making up your own pages, the same procedure should, of course, be followed.

fig 34

A pocket inside the front cover for photographs or other items to be pasted in the book is sometimes useful. Such a pocket can be made by cutting a piece of tooling calf leather of the right size and shape, skiving the bottom and two sides, and cementing or stitching the skived edges to the inner side of the cover. (See Fig. 34.)

LADY'S HAND PURSE

Fig. 35 illustrates a hand purse that is of convenient size and design and has only three parts—an outside cover, a piece to form an inner pocket, and a small handle. It should be made either of calfskin or cowhide tooling leather. The piece of leather for the cover should measure 6½ by 11½ inches; that for the pocket 6½ by 6½ inches; and the handle 6½ by 1¼ inches. Cut the pieces as shown in the drawing.

When the pieces have been cut out, attach the two parts of the snap fastener. The lower part of the large piece of leather folds upward on the line indicated to form a pocket, and the positions of the two parts of the fastener can be determined by folding along this line and then folding down the curved top part of the leather. While the bottom part of the leather is folded up, the holes for lacing may be punched. Punch through both thicknesses of leather at the same time, where the leather overlaps, so that the holes will exactly coincide. Be careful, also, to have the holes in the inner flap, which forms a second pocket, coincide with the holes in the cover piece.

Skive the lower edge of the inner flap, and cement it to the cover piece. Then place the handle in position on the outside of the cover

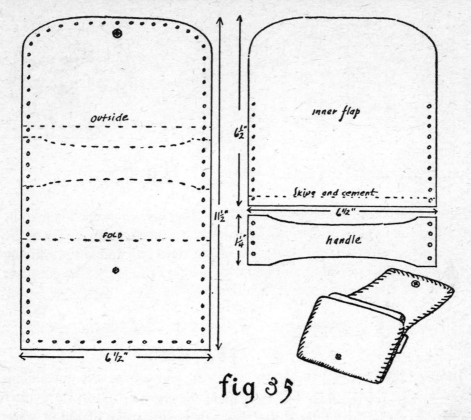

fig 35

piece, fold up the bottom part of the cover, and lace the parts together. Note that the upper part of the inner flap is not punched for lacing. This part forms a flap or cover for the inner pocket which is made by cementing the bottom edge of this piece to the cover. When the bag is completed, it has two pockets, an outer and an inner one.

This type of purse may be left plain or may be decorated with a tooled or stamped design. If a design is used, the tooling or stamping should be done before the parts are assembled.

LADY'S COMBINATION PURSE AND CARD CASE

A COMBINATION purse and card case of the type shown in Fig. 36 makes an exceptionally useful and attractive gift, and is not difficult to make. You will need four pieces of calf tooling leather of the following dimensions for the purse illustrated: 3½ by 5 inches, for the cover; 3½

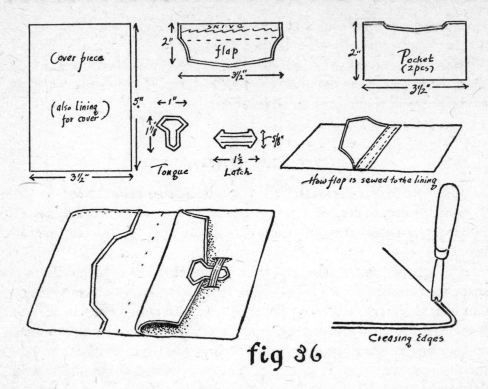

fig 36

by 2 inches, for the flap; 1⅛ by 1 inch, for the tongue; and 1½ by ⅝ inch, for the latch. Other materials needed are a piece of lining leather measuring 3½ by 5 inches, with which to line the cover, and two additional pieces, each 3½ by 2 inches, for the pockets.

First cut the tooling leather and the two pockets to the sizes and shapes shown in the drawing, or slightly larger, as they may have to be trimmed a little after sewing. Then dampen the cover, if it is to be tooled, and tool on it the design you have chosen for the purpose. Tool lines along the edges of the flap, tongue, and latch, and the inner edges of the two pockets, as shown. These lines can be made with a modeling tool guided by a ruler or steel straightedge.

Now, following the drawing, cement the tongue to the edge of the flap, and then stitch the tongue in place, using a sewing machine with silk thread and a fine needle. The thread should be about the same color as the leather. Skive the straight edge of the flap, fold it over on the dotted line, and cement it to the 3½ by 5 inch piece of lining leather. Then sew the flap to the lining. Follow by cementing and sewing the two pockets to the lining, and at the same time sewing the lining to the 3 ½ by 5 inch piece of tooling leather which forms the cover of the purse.

Complete the purse by skiving the ends of the latch and cementing them inside slits cut in the pocket to receive them. Then crease the edges of the purse all round with an edge creaser.

A MINIATURE INDIAN TEPEE

GOATSKIN is recommended for the little Indian tepee shown in Fig. 37, since it reproduces the appearance of many of the original tepees. However, various other soft leathers, such as suede or calfskin may be used.

Cut a paper pattern first and trim it until it is just the right size and shape to permit the front edges of the tepee to meet closely and evenly. Cut out the leather, according to the pattern, and punch holes in the two front edges so that they can be laced together. Then mount the tepee on four or five small sticks brought together and bound with string near their tops, as shown in the drawing. The two pointed pieces of leather at the top of the tepee may need reinforcing or stiffening with pieces of cardboard cemented to their backs if they do not stand upright of their own accord.

The tepee should be decorated with Indian designs painted on with thin oil paints or leather dyes. Such designs are obtainable in great variety from all leathercraft supply dealers.

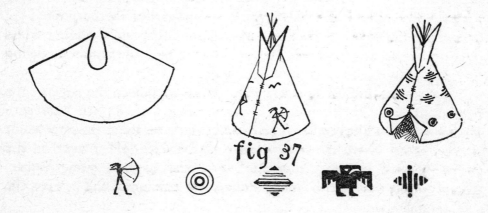

fig 37

A DRAWSTRING BAG

BAGS of the type shown in Fig. 38 are easy to make and are very convenient for shopping, carrying knitting materials or sewing, and many other purposes. Suede leather is suggested as the most suitable material.

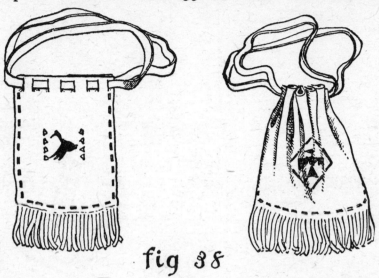

fig 38

Two rectangular pieces are cut out, one for the front and one for the back. Each piece should be long enough to include the leather needed for the bottom fringe. Dimensions may be varied according to individual preference, but a good sized bag for most purposes is one measuring about 12 inches deep and 10 inches wide. If an extra 5 inches is allowed for the fringe, the front and back pieces should then measure 17 by 10 inches.

Cut the fringes with a pair of shears and then join the two pieces together with broad suede lacing, using the running stitch shown in the drawing. Make the slits for the drawstrings, and insert the strings, which are made of strips of suede about three-quarters of an inch wide.

Bags of this type may be decorated with stenciled designs or with bead work.

A BILLFOLD WITH STAMP POCKETS

IT IS best to sew this billfold, which is made of tooling calf of medium weight and thickness. Note that the outside or cover piece is a little wider than the two pocket pieces. This is to enable the case to fold easily without creasing on the inside.

After the pieces have been cut out, the small pocket and the stamp

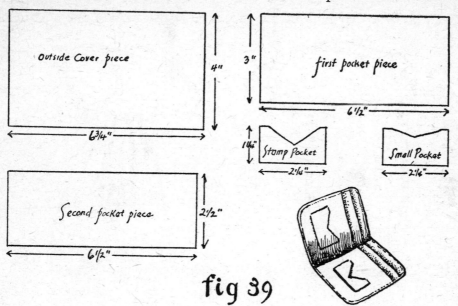

Outside Cover piece 4" 6¾"

3" *first pocket piece* 6½"

1¼" *Stamp Pocket* 2¼" *Small Pocket* 2¼"

Second pocket piece 2½" 6½"

fig 39

pocket are sewn onto the inner or second pocket piece. Then the first and second pockets are placed on top of the outside cover piece and are sewed together. Begin the sewing down one of the side edges and continue to within one-half inch of the center of the bottom edge. Fasten off and start sewing again where you first began, working around the top of the billfold and down the other side edge, including the side edges of the first and second pocket pieces. Continue to within one-half inch of the center of the bottom edge as before and fasten off. This method of sewing helps to make the case fold easily and without creasing or bulging.

A LONG BILLFOLD

THE outside of this billfold, or the piece marked A, should be made of medium-weight black or brown tooling calf. The three inside pieces, B, C, D, are made of calf lining leather. (See Fig. 40.)

Make a paper pattern for each piece shown in the drawing and cut out the four pieces of leather. The large piece, A, which forms the outside of the billfold, is larger than piece B, which goes on the inside, to allow for the folding of the leather. Piece A may be left plain or may be decorated by means of a tooled border, a monogram, or some other form of decoration. An opening or window is cut out of the small piece, C, and a piece of celluloid or cellophane is cemented to the back of the piece. The right-hand edge of this piece is then laced to give it greater sturdiness.

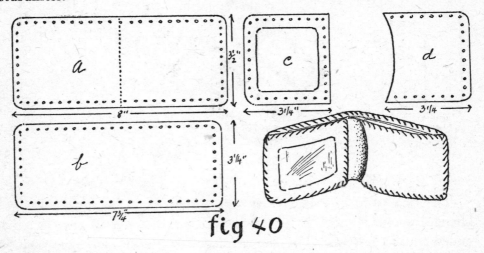

fig 40

Punch holes in each piece, as indicated in the drawing. Then lace the upper edges of pieces C and D to the upper edge of piece B. Next put piece B on piece A and lace all the parts together. The bottom edges of pieces A and B should coincide, and this means that the top edge of B will not reach to the top edge of A. The lacing is started, therefore, one hole down from the top edge of A, on the left-hand side, and is passed through the topmost hole in piece B. The lacing goes down the left-hand side, across the bottom edge, and up the right-hand side. It is then continued to the left across the top edge of piece A to provide uniformity.

A SEWING KIT

Suede or calfskin may be used for the useful little sewing kit illustrated in Fig. 41. It is made of two pieces of leather, one to form the base of the kit, and one to make the sectionalized pocket that holds the scissors, tape measure, and packet of needles. The case may be unlined or, if preferred, may be lined with skiver cemented to the base piece.

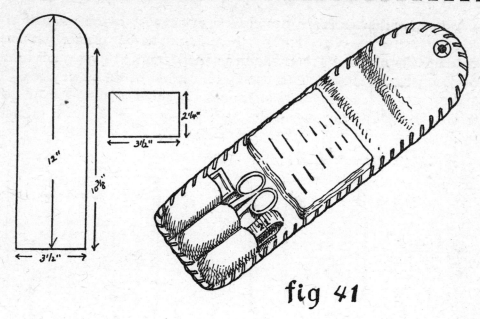

fig 41

The two parts may be joined together either by lacing or sewing. The end pocket, however, must be sewed on each side of the space intended for the scissors. The flannel piece for needles and pins may be either stitched or cemented to the base piece of leather. As shown in the drawing, the kit is fastened shut with a snap fastener.

A CIGARETTE CASE

CIGARETTE cases of the type shown in Fig. 42 may be made of thin tooling calf, of suede, or of reptile skin.

The paper pattern for the case is made by fitting a piece of paper around a package of cigarettes. Allow ¾₁₆ of an inch extra on each side of the body of the pattern for lacing. Pieces of lining leather should be cemented to the inside of the two side panels, and also on the inside of the front of the case where the slits are made to hold the end of the flap. Cut along the lines a-b and c-d. This makes it possible to fold the bottom into position. The two tabs formed by the cut are later glued to the sides of the case.

A stamped border, which may be gold-leafed, makes an effective

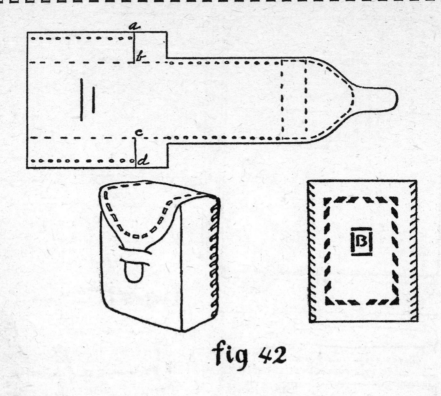

fig 42

decoration for the back of the case. In the center a small decorative figure, either tooled or stamped, can be placed.

To assemble the case, simply lace the back to the two side panels, using whichever type of lacing you prefer. The running stitch shown on the flap in the drawing makes an attractive finish to this part of the case.

A BRIEF CASE

THE brief case illustrated in Fig. 43 may be made of brown or black calfskin. It consists of three main pieces of leather—one for the back and flap, one for the gusset, and one for the front. In addition, smaller pieces of calfskin are needed for the handle and its two fastenings, and for the flap strap and buckle straps.

Cut out the leather pieces according to the shapes and dimensions shown in the drawings. Sew the front piece to the gusset, and then sew

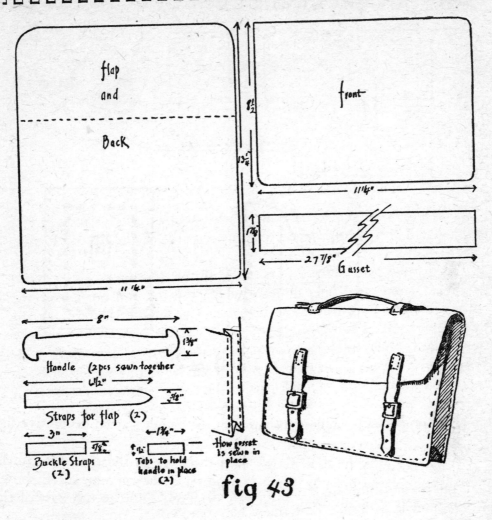

fig 43

the back piece to the opposite edge of the gusset. The handle is double, the two pieces being sewn together all around the edge.

Two pieces of each of the smaller items will be needed. These are the small pieces for fastening the handle, the two straps for the flap, and the two straps that fasten the buckles to the front of the case. These pieces, when ready, are sewed to the body of the case in the positions clearly indicated in the drawing.

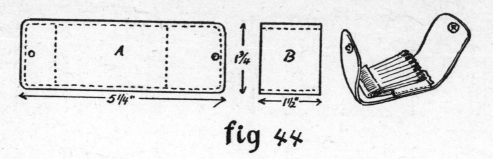

fig 44

A CONTAINER FOR BOOK MATCHES

THIS container should be made of thin tooling calf. It may be left undecorated or can be stamped with a decorative figure, dyed or gold-leafed.

Cut a paper pattern for the cover, A, to the dimensions given in the drawing. The dotted lines indicate where the top and bottom of the cover are to be folded over the matches. Cut another pattern for the smaller piece, B. The side edges of this piece are cemented, sewed, or laced with running stitching to the sides of the center section of piece A. When the container is in use, the front of the cover of a packet of book matches is torn off and the back part of the cover is inserted underneath the pocket piece, B. After piece B has been fastened in place, the container is completed by adding a snap fastener.

A DOUBLE PICTURE FRAME

THIS is a small folding frame designed to hold two snapshots or small pictures, one in each side. The frame will stand upright on a table or can be carried, folded, in a handbag.

Medium-thickness tooling calf is a good leather to use, if a design is to be tooled or stamped on the cover of the frame. Sheepskin, which is less expensive, can be used if no tooling is to be done. (Sheepskin is not generally used for tooling as it is too soft. "Tooling sheepskin" may be purchased, however, and can be successfully tooled if the work is done slowly and carefully.)

Draw and cut out paper patterns for the cover, A, and for the two identical inside frames, B. The dimensions given can, of course, be changed to make the frame any desired size and shape.

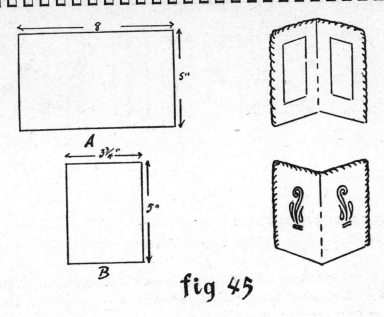

fig 45

Cut the leather according to the patterns. The openings in the frame pieces, B, should be cut with a very sharp knife or a razor blade, so the edges of the leather will be clean-cut. A piece of transparent celluloid or cellophane is glued to the back of each piece.

Before lacing the two frame pieces to the cover, the cover may be lined, if desired, with a piece of silk.

The outside of the cover may be left plain or may be decorated with a tooled or tooled and stamped design, either the one shown in the drawing or one purchased from a leathercraft supply dealer. Dyes or other coloring may be used according to individual taste.

A PHOTOGRAPH FRAME

MANY different types and designs of leather frames for photographs, both large and small, can be made by leathercraft workers. The frame shown in Fig. 46 is one of the most popular kinds. Frames of this type can be made of different colored leathers and with a plain or elaborately decorated cover, according to individual taste.

For the frame illustrated, you will need one large piece of tooling calfskin measuring 8¾ by 5¾ inches; two pieces of calf suede lining leather, each 4⅛ by 5¾ inches; two cardboard stiffening pieces, each

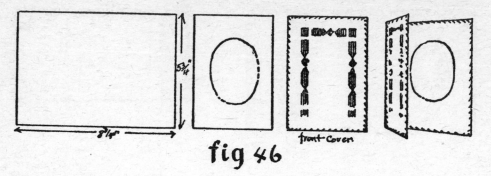

fig 46

4⅛ by 5¾ inches, to put between the outer calfskin and the lining pieces; and leather lacing.

The design to be used is transferred to the part of the calfskin that is to form the front cover of the folded frame, and is carried out by means of tooling, stamping, or one of the other methods of leather decoration. When the design has been completed, holes for lacing are punched around all four edges of the leather.

One piece of the suede lining leather is left untouched after it has been cut out, but a rectangular or oval opening is cut in the other piece.

To assemble the frame, place the cardboard stiffening pieces on the calfskin, with their outside edges coinciding with the left and right-hand edges of the leather. This leaves a ½-inch space between the inner edges of the cardboard pieces. Place the two pieces of lining leather over the cardboard pieces and punch holes for lacing through both the cardboard and the suede. These holes must, of course, coincide with those previously punched in the calfskin. Then lace all around the edge of the calfskin. When this has been done, the two sides of the lining toward the center will be unlaced. The right-hand one should be left open to permit the insertion of the photograph, and the left-hand edge should be cemented to the calfskin.

A DESK OR BLOTTER PAD

DESK or blotter pads are among the most popular of leathercraft articles, and can be made without difficulty. Fig. 47 shows one that can be made in a comparatively short time and without much experience in leatherwork.

The size depends upon individual preference or upon the size of the

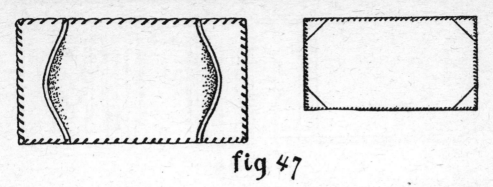

fig 47

desk on which the pad is to be used, so no measurements are given in the drawing. The first step is to cut a piece of heavy cardboard to the size determined upon for the pad. To each side of the cardboard cement a piece of sheep skiver.

Next cut pieces of calfskin or cowhide to form the two end pieces. These may be of the shape shown in the drawing or a modification of this shape. The end pieces may be left plain or may be decorated with tooled lines near the border, as shown in the drawing, or with some more elaborate tooled or stamped design.

If desired, the end pieces may be omitted, and four triangular-shaped corner pieces used instead. If corner pieces are used, they may be decorated or left plain.

To assemble the pad, put the end or corner pieces in position, punch holes for lacing, and lace all the pieces together.

A BOOK COVER

THE measurements given below for the book cover shown in Fig. 48 are to fit a standard-sized novel. They may, of course, be altered to fit any book.

Tooling calf or cowhide leathers are suitable for this type of article. Three pieces of leather are needed, one for the outer cover, which should measure 12¾ by 8½ inches, and two identical pieces, measuring 3¾ by 8½ inches. These are to be laced to the cover piece to form two pockets into which the covers of the book are slipped. All the edges to be laced together should first be skived down to one-half their original thickness.

Any design that suits your individual taste may be used for the outer

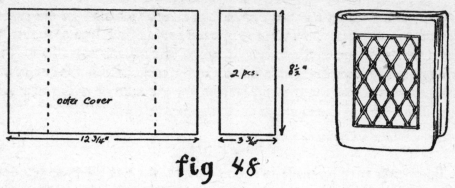

fig 48

cover. Many covers are finished simply with a border made with an embossing wheel or stamps, and gold-leafed, or with such a border and a decorative medallion or other figure tooled or stamped and gold-leafed in the center of the front of the cover.

When the design has been completed, tool two lines in the center back of the cover, on the inside, to permit the cover to fold neatly around the back of the book without wrinkling.

A SINGLE-PIECE BOOK COVER

Book covers are frequently made from a single piece of leather. (Fig. 49.) The single piece is long enough to form the outer cover that goes

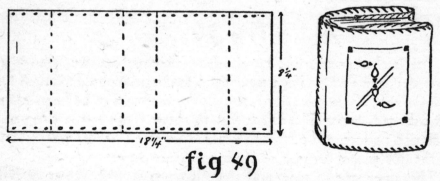

fig 49

over the back and covers of the book, and also to form the two end pieces, or pockets, into which the covers of the book are slipped.

Make a paper pattern that fits the book for which the cover is intended. Be sure to allow a little extra length to provide for the loss in folding, due to the thickness of the leather, and also for the margins required for lacing.

When the design has been tooled, stamped, stenciled, or otherwise brought to completion, the top and bottom edges of the leather should be skived where the pockets are to be joined to the outside cover part. The lacing not only joins the folded-in ends to the main part of the cover, but is also carried across the top and bottom for the sake of uniformity and durability. Any of the methods of lacing may be used.

BOOK ENDS

Book ends may be made in several shapes, such as the rounded ones shown in Fig. 50, or they may be rectangular, or with sides that curve in to a point at the top. Any one of the numerous suitable designs that can be purchased from leathercraft supply dealers may be used, or you can make up your own design.

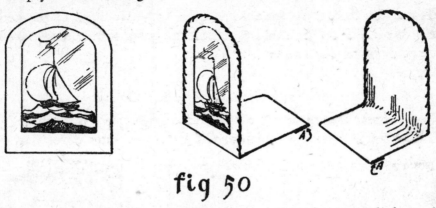

fig 50

The leather ends are to be glued or cemented to two light-weight galvanized iron pieces. Each piece has a flat bottom section and, at right angles to this, a side (the part to which the leather is to be fastened) cut to the desired shape. The easiest way to obtain these pieces is to make a cardboard pattern and take it to a hardware store, where they will cut out the iron pieces for you, according to your pattern.

The inner side of each end piece is covered with skiver or lining leather. Cut a paper pattern for the lining and allow an extra inch to be folded underneath the end of the bottom section, as at *a* in the drawing. Fasten the lining to the end pieces with glue or cement.

Cut the outside leather end pieces so that they will extend ¼ of an inch beyond the sides and tops of the iron pieces. This is to provide room for finishing with lacing.

The design on the outside leather end pieces may be tooled, incised, stenciled or outlined by hot-point work, and the leather used may be natural color or commercially dyed. When the design has been completed, lace around the edges of each end piece, and then glue the leather pieces to the iron frames.

A WATCH STAND

THIS watch stand is both useful and attractive and is easy to make. It holds a watch in a leather frame which can stand on a desk, dresser or table.

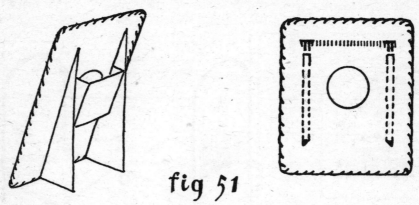

fig 51

The framework, with supports to hold it upright and a compartment to hold the watch, is made of stiff cardboard parts fastened together with glue and gummed sealing tape. It should be covered with skiver, lining leather or heavy silk.

The front of the frame is covered with a square piece of tooling calf, either natural color or already dyed an attractive color. It is laced to the cardboard frame. Make a paper pattern of the right size, cut out the leather, and then tool or stamp the design chosen on the leather, if a design is being used. The circular opening for the watch face should be very carefully cut out with a sharp knife or a razor blade.

When the design has been completed, the leather is laced to the front of the cardboard frame, using any one of the methods of lacing. It may be necessary to add an extra piece of cardboard between the leather and the front of the frame to give added strength, and this can be determined by one's individual judgment. If this extra piece is needed, it should be cut to the same size and shape as the leather piece and should have a similar circular opening in the center.

A SCHOOL BAG

THE school bag illustrated in Fig. 52 is made of three pieces of brown calfskin—one piece for the back and the flap, one for the front, and one for the gusset which joins the front piece to the back. In addition to these main pieces, other smaller pieces of calfskin will be needed for the shoulder straps, flap straps, and buckle straps.

Cut out the leather pieces according to the shapes and dimensions

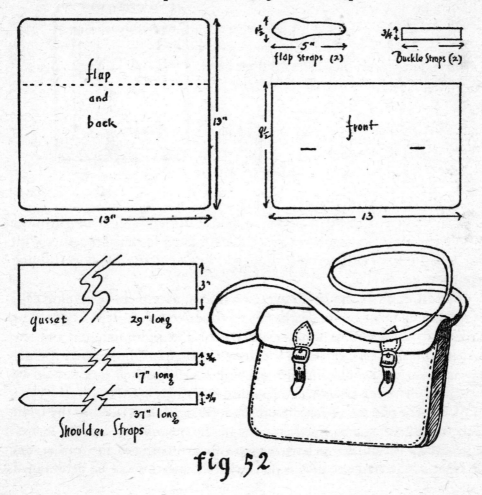

fig 52

shown in the drawings. Sew the front piece to the gusset, and then sew the back piece to the opposite edge of the gusset. The two straps which, when buckled together at their centers, form the shoulder strap, are sewed to the top edges of the gusset. The flap straps and buckle straps (which hold the buckles to the bag) are then sewed in place, and the bag is completed.

A NECKERCHIEF SLIDE

Boy Scouts and others who wear neckerchiefs, as part of a cowboy outfit or for other reasons, can use a leather neckerchief slide of this Western cowboy type. It is made from a piece of strap leather measuring 3½ by 1¼ inches.

Bevel the ends of the leather with a cutting knife, and then punch the holes for lacing. The decoration may be done by tooling, stamping or hot-point work. The lacing is done as shown in the drawings, the ends of the lacing passing between the inner and outer loops.

fig 53

A PENCIL CASE

PENCIL cases of the kind illustrated in Fig. 54 are frequently made of pigskin, and this type of leather is recommended. Cut the leather according to the pattern and dimensions shown in the drawing. Next cut two pieces of cardboard, each 7¼ by 1¾ inches. These are to serve as stiffening pieces beneath the pencils, and are covered with skiver leather cemented in place. Using a sewing machine, sew a strap made of pigskin to the center of each covered piece of cardboard, making four loops on each to hold pencils and pens.

Next fix the socket or bottom part of the snap fastener in place. Its position is indicated by the dot on the pattern. It is fastened on the out-

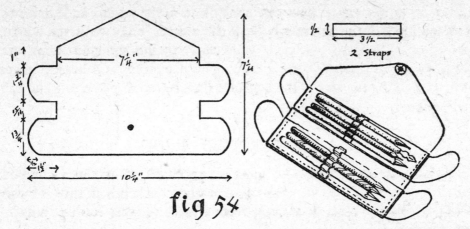

fig 54

side of the leather. Sew the two leather-covered pieces of cardboard in position on the pigskin, as shown in the illustration. The one that covers the bottom part of the snap fastener is sewn at the ends and along the outer edge, but the other one need only be sewn at the ends.

Fold up the case, determine where the top part of the snap fastener should be put, and fix it in position to complete the case.

LOOSE LEAF MEMO BOOK COVER

THE memo book shown in Fig. 55 is of the type that may be purchased, with plain covers, at any ten-cent store. The tooled leather cover is added by the craftsman.

The covering is made of tooling calf and is cut the same size and shape as the cover of the memo book. After the design has been traced and tooled or stamped, the cover is pasted to the original cover of the memo

fig 55

book, and is then laced around the edges. Punch the holes for lacing ⅛ of an inch in from the edges and space them closer together at the corners than along the straight edges, or else pass the lacing through one hole two or three times at each of the corners.

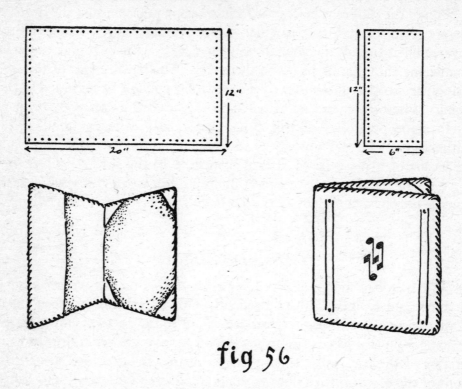

fig 56

WRITING PORTFOLIO

The handsome writing portfolio shown in Fig. 56 may be made of tooling calf or cowhide, and may be given either a simple or elaborate stamped or tooled design, according to individual taste. Natural-color or commercially-dyed leather, such as dark green, may be used.

The cover is made from a single piece of leather, measuring approximately 12 by 20 inches, although these measurements may be altered considerably in order to make a portfolio for a certain-sized desk or in accordance with individual preference. Cut out the leather for the cover, and decorate it with the design you have chosen, using tooling or one of the other methods already described in executing the design.

Next cut out a piece of leather measuring 12 by 6 inches to form a pocket on the inside of the front cover. You will also need four triangular pieces, which are to be laced to the four corners of the back cover to hold a blotter in place.

Punch the different pieces for lacing, making certain that the holes in the pocket piece and the triangular pieces coincide with the holes in the cover. Then lace all the way around the edges of the cover, at the same time lacing the separate pieces to the cover. The inside edges of the two triangular pieces at the center of the portfolio will not be included in this lacing. They are therefore fastened to the cover by means of cement.

In some portfolios of this type, particularly when a light-weight leather is used for the cover, it is advisable to stiffen the right-hand side by means of a piece of cardboard cemented to the leather. Over this piece is cemented a piece of skiver or lining leather of the same dimensions as the right-hand half of the portfolio.

LADY'S HANDBAG

THE handbag shown in Fig. 57 is made of tooling calf, either natural or dyed, and is lined with colored skiver or lining leather. It is made from a single piece of leather, cut according to the pattern shown in the drawing. To this piece, gussets are added to give greater fullness to the interior of the bag, and a small piece of leather is laced into slits in the front of the bag to form a slot for the pointed tab. This small piece is cut 1¼ inches wide and is folded double to a width of ⅝ of an inch before being fastened in place.

A simple design or monogram may be tooled on the flap, and the simplest type of lacing—the running stitch—is used for the lacing, which is clearly shown in the illustration.

COMBINATION MEMORANDUM PAD
AND COIN PURSE

CALFSKIN or cowhide may be used for this combination purse and memorandum pad which can be used for jotting down errands, addresses, telephone numbers, and so forth. The dimensions may vary according to choice or according to the size of the memorandum pad that is to be used. (See Fig. 58.)

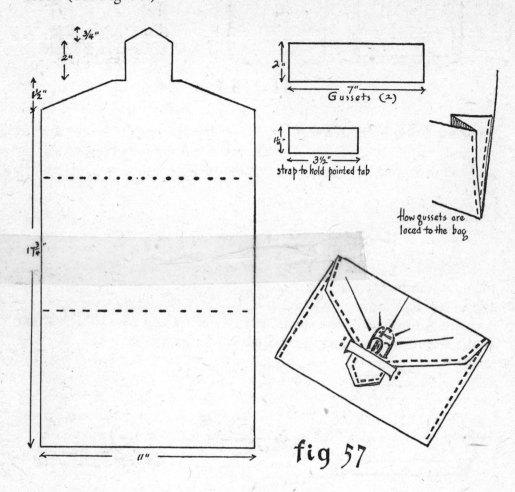

fig 57

The cover consists of a piece of calfskin, plain or decorated with a tooled or stamped design. This is lined with a piece of skiver of the same dimensions, cemented in place. The small coin purse should be made separately and should be stitched to the lining before the latter is cemented to the cover piece. The purse is made of two pieces of calfskin, one for the back and the flap, and the other for the front. These are sewed together.

To the left-hand side of the lining cement a piece of calfskin to form a pocket to hold the cardboard back of the memorandum pad. Then ce-

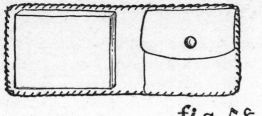

fig 58

ment the lining to the cover piece, smoothing it from the center toward the ends to prevent bulging. Complete the case by punching for lacing and lacing around the edges, starting the lacing at the center of the top edge.

A VELLUM LAMPSHADE

THE lampshade shown in Fig. 59 is made of calfskin vellum or parchment, a translucent material which gives a soft diffused light. A wire frame will have to be purchased at a ten-cent store or department store, and the dimensions of the shade will be determined by the size of the frame and the type of lamp for which it is intended.

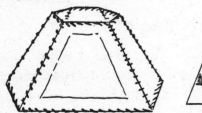
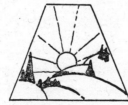

fig 59

The shade is made of six pieces of vellum, all cut to the same size and shape, as shown in the drawing. The edges are punched for lacing; the six sections are laced together, and the top and bottom edges are also laced.

Vellum can be decorated by means of colored inks, oil paint well thinned out with turpentine, or leather dyes.

A CIRCULAR LAMPSHADE

THIS lampshade is also made of vellum and may be decorated with oil paints, dyes or colored inks. Since it is difficult to draw and measure freehand the exact shape of the piece that is to be cut out, a paper pattern should be made and should be adjusted until the top and bottom edges of the shade meet evenly when the two ends are brought together.

The ends may either be overlapped and stitched together, or may be joined by lacing. The size of the shade will be determined by the size of the wire frame around which it is to fit.

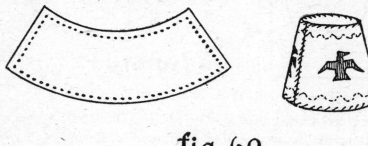

fig 60

A CASE FOR MEN'S BRUSHES

THIS case, designed to hold a pair of men's hair brushes, is made from three pieces of calfskin—one for the back and the flap, one for the front, and one for the gusset that attaches the front to the back. In addition, two pieces of lining leather will be needed to line the two pieces that form the back and the flap and the front. The dimensions given in the drawings will make a case that will fit the average-sized pair of brushes, but may be altered for brushes that are either larger or smaller. The pieces are sewn together, and the case is fastened by means of two snap fasteners. (See Fig. 61.)

Sew the gusset to the front piece first, and then to complete the outside of the case, sew the back piece to the other edge of the gusset. The two pieces of lining leather are pasted to the inside surfaces of the front and back pieces when the assembly of the case has been completed.

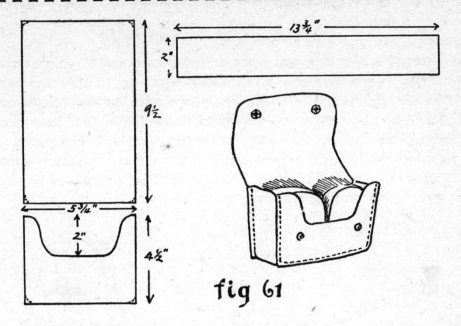

fig 61

If preferred, the gusset may be laced to the front and back pieces. If this is done, the lacing should be continued on around the flap that forms the upper part of the back piece.

LEATHER BELTS

IT IS possible to make a large number of different kinds of leather belts, all of which are attractive and easy to make. The best known kind is probably the carved or stamped leather belt, which consists of a solid leather strap decorated with an incised or carved design or stamped with a series of repetitive figures. (See No. 1, Fig. 62.) Belt straps for belts of this type can be purchased, already cut, from leathercraft supply dealers, or you may cut your own strap from cowhide or calfskin. Use cowhide for deep incising, and calfskin for tooling. Belt buckles can also be purchased from leathercraft dealers.

When you have your strap, the first thing to do is to fasten on the buckle. Measure back about 2 inches from one end of the strap and cut a round hole in the middle of the strap for the tongue of the buckle to pass through. Next punch six holes in a straight line across the strap, close to where the back of the buckle will be, and punch corresponding holes in the 2-inch long piece that is to be folded back against the strap to hold the buckle in place. Make similar corresponding holes near the end of the folded-back piece and the belt strap.

Put the tongue of the buckle through the hole that was punched for it, fold back the 2-inch long piece, and lace through the row of holes closest to the buckle. Then lace through the second row of holes.

Cut a narrow strip of leather to form the belt loop. It should be about ⅜ of an inch wide and long enough to fit loosely around the strap. Punch holes in both ends of this piece, and fasten the ends together by means of a piece of strong thin cord passed through the holes. Slip the loop over the end of the belt opposite to the buckle, and move it up close to the buckle.

Punch holes for the buckle tongue in the end of the belt opposite to the buckle. Eyelets may be inserted in these holes, if desired.

The belt may be decorated by means of incising, stamping, or tooling, using any design that suits your taste. Before applying the design, dampen the leather and crease the two edges of the strap with an edge creaser.

Belt No. 2 in Fig. 62 is a two-color woman's belt made of suede and fastened by means of two snap fasteners. It is best to cut a paper pattern for this belt because of its increased width in the front, which must be drawn and cut out symmetrically. The main part of the belt is of a dark color and one or more lighter colors are used for the decoration. The decorative figures are glued or cemented in place. Two narrow strips of suede run around the belt, one on each edge. These are cut so the pointed fastening tabs are a part of each strip, and are securely glued or cemented in place.

Belt No. 3 is made of a number of pieces of calfskin cut to the two shapes, A and B, shown in the drawing. These are sewn together, and the number of pieces used depends upon the length of the belt. The belt is designed to be made in two colors—dark brown for the A pieces, for example, and natural-color or undyed calfskin for the B pieces.

Dampen each piece and, with a tracing tool, make lines parallel to the edges. Then cut two slits in each B piece, as indicated in the draw-

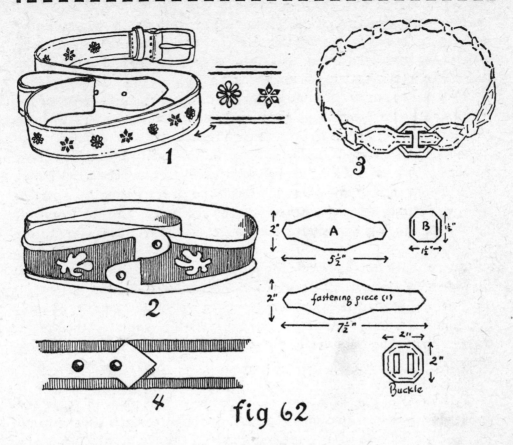

fig 62

ing. The ends of the A pieces are passed through these slits, then turned back and sewed. The special fastening piece is sewed to one of the B pieces in the same way. It should be strengthened by gluing or cementing another piece of calfskin to the back.

The buckle is made of five pieces of leather to give it the needed strength. These pieces are glued or cemented together and are then slotted as shown in the drawing. The end of one of the A pieces is passed through one of the slots, turned back on itself, and sewed.

An interesting but simply made suede leather belt is No. 4. Cut the leather 2½ inches wide, and cut one end to a point. Then fold over each edge for a distance of ⅜ of an inch, hammer these parts down, and glue them to the main part of the belt. The belt is completed by attaching two snap fasteners as shown in the drawing.

A KNIFE SHEATH

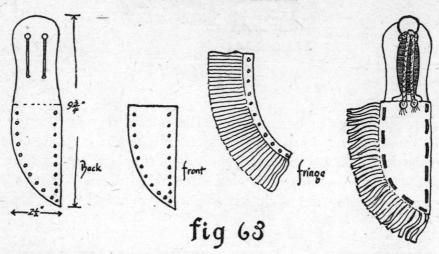

back   front   fringe

fig 63

Tooling calf leather is the best material to use for the fringed knife sheath shown in Fig. 63. Make paper patterns according to the measurements given in the drawings, or to fit the knife for which the sheath is to be used, and cut out the two leather pieces that form the sheath. Two slits are cut in the back piece to allow the sheath to be slipped onto a belt, and two circular holes are punched or cut at the upper ends of the slits to hold a small strap or cord to tie around the knife to keep it from dropping from the sheath.

The fringe is made of tooling calf leather, the fringes being cut with a sharp knife or razor blade. When it is completed, punch holes for lacing, as indicated in the drawing, and lace the three parts of the sheath together, using the simple running stitch.

SUITCASE NAME TAG

This suitcase tag, which holds a calling card or other card bearing the name of the owner, is made from calfskin or cowhide. Two pieces of leather of the same shape and size are cut out to form the front and the back of the tag, and a window or opening is cut out of the front piece with a sharp knife or a razor blade. A stamped or tooled design may be executed around the opening.

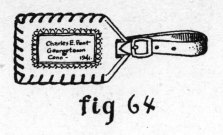

fig 64

Skive the edges of both pieces and lace them together around the three straight edges. Then cement a piece of transparent celluloid inside to cover the window. The strap is made from a piece of strap leather. A buckle is fastened to one end by sewing the end of the strap to the standing part, and holes for the buckle tongue are punched in the opposite end.

fig 65

LEATHER PICTURE PLAQUES

LEATHER picture plaques of the kind shown in Fig. 65 are made by cementing pieces of thin leather to a background piece, which may be a piece of stiff leather or a piece of heavy cardboard over which has been cemented a piece of thin leather. Commercially-dyed leathers of different colors are suitable for this kind of work and can be obtained in all the needed shades, such as blue for the sky, green for grass and trees, white for clouds, and so on. Some workers, however, prefer to use natural color leather, which they color by means of dyes or oil paints after the picture has been assembled.

Suggestions for pictures may be obtained from many sources or, if you are artistically inclined, you can devise your own pictures. Popular pictures that are quite widely used are those copied from children's books in which fairy tales and the Mother Goose rhymes are simply but brightly illustrated.

When a picture has been chosen, all the parts should be cut out, carefully assembled, and cemented to the background The plaque may be finished off by making a frame of narrow leather strips around the border, or by lacing the border.

BUNNY SLIPPERS

CHILDREN are very fond of these slippers and they make wonderful presents that will be sure to be appreciated.

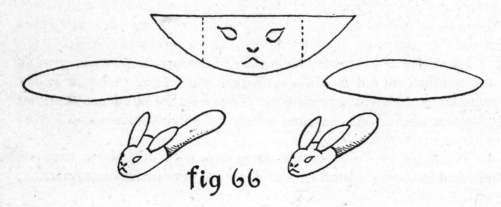

fig 66

Four pieces of soft leather are needed for each slipper—one slightly thicker and heavier than the others for the sole, and the other three for the upper toe pieces and the bunny's ears. Measure the length and width of the child's feet and cut the soles of the slippers to fit them. The correct size for the toe pieces is obtained by measuring the thickness of the foot just above the toes. The shape of the toe pieces is shown in the drawing. Make them slightly larger all around the edge nearest the sole to allow for sewing or lacing them to the soles.

The eyes and nose of the bunny may be painted on, outlined with colored threads, or made of small beads sewed to the soft leather. The ears are cut from soft leather and are sewed in place, and the slippers are then completed by sewing or lacing the toe pieces to the soles.

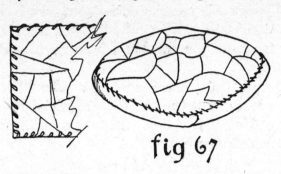

fig 67

PATCHWORK PILLOW COVERS

SCRAPS of brightly-colored suede or lining leather, when sewed together in attractive patchwork designs, make good-looking and out-of-the-ordinary pillow covers. The back of the cover may be made either of suede or sheepskin, or both sides may have a patchwork design.

First make a full-size drawing of the patchwork design you intend to use, and then cut out the different shaped and colored pieces of leather required to make up the patchwork. The pieces are best joined together by means of a sewing machine, which will stitch through thin leather without any difficulty.

When the two sides of the cover have been completed, they are punched for lacing around all four edges and are then laced together.

MOCCASINS

MOCCASINS are usually made of suede or velvet finished split cowhide today, since the buckskin formerly used by the Indians is quite difficult to obtain.

The first step is to trace on a piece of paper the outlines of the feet of the person for whom the moccasins are intended. When the tracings are completed, cut out each one with a pair of scissors, to serve as a guide when making the pattern for the moccasins. Draw on each outline the

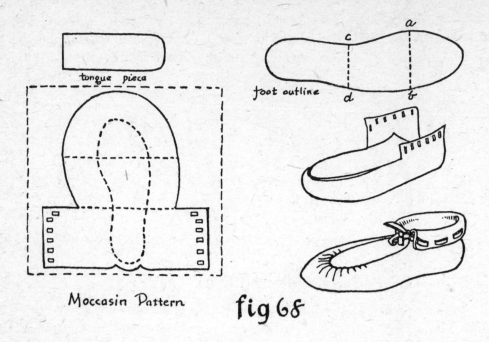

tongue piece

foot outline

Moccasin Pattern

fig 68

lines A-B and C-D. Place the right foot outline on a rectangular piece of paper, as indicated by the dotted outline in the drawing. Extend the lines A-B and C-D, as shown by the dotted lines. Mark the toe portion of the pattern outline around and parallel to the outlines of the front portion of the foot.

Next make a paper pattern for the tongue piece. The width of the tongue is two-thirds the length of the line A-B. Its exact length is best determined by experimenting with the paper pattern. Cut the pattern 2 or 3 inches longer than the estimated length and then, by fitting it in place with the other pattern, determine the exact correct length.

The patterns for the left-foot moccasin are made in the same way as those for the right.

The moccasins should be assembled inside out, and later reversed. Stitch the tongue piece to the sole piece with linen thread, or lace the two pieces together, according to your preference. When completed, a leather thong is passed through holes made for that purpose in the part of the moccasin surrounding the ankle.

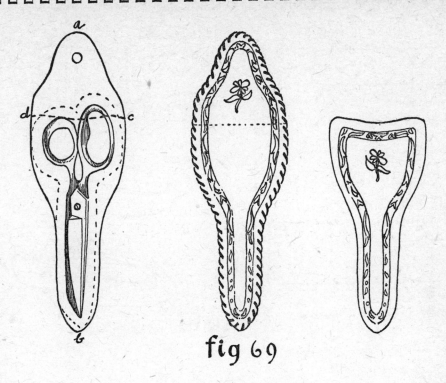

fig 69

A SCISSORS CASE

THE scissors case shown in Fig. 69 may be made of tooling calf, cowhide or steerhide. The size of the leather needed will depend upon the size of the scissors or shears for which the case is intended.

Make a pattern by placing the scissors on a piece of paper and tracing around them, and then making a second outline ⅜ of an inch outside the first to provide room for the lacing. The second outline is indicated by the light dotted line in the drawing. Fold the paper on the center line, A-B, and cut out a symmetrical pattern of the shape shown in the illustration. The flap should be about one-third the length of the scissors. Transfer the pattern to the leather, and cut out the leather.

A second piece of leather is now cut out to form the top or front part of the case. It is the same shape as the first piece, but is not so long, reaching only to the heavy dotted line shown in the drawing.

The design may be tooled or stamped, and should be applied so as to leave a margin of ¼ inch or more for the lacing. When the leather has dried after being decorated, cement the edges of the two pieces of leather together, and then punch holes for lacing about ⅛ inch in from the edge. The holes should be made closer together around the curved parts than along the straight edges.

Start the lacing at C, and continue all the way around the case. When the lacing has been completed, punch a hole in the flap for the cap of a snap fastener. Then put the scissors in the case, fold the flap over, and mark the position of the hole for the post of the fastener. The insertion of the snap fastener completes the case.

LEATHER COVERED BOXES

ORDINARY wooden boxes may be transformed into very beautiful articles by covering them with leather, decorated with tooled or stamped designs, and either left uncolored or accentuated by dyes or gold leaf. Small wooden boxes of varying sizes and shapes can be obtained at ten-cent stores and department stores; and similar boxes, which have been used for packaging, are frequently to be found in one's own house or in the homes of friends.

Thin tooling calf, steerhide, cowhide, goatskin, sheepskin, and suede are all used for covering boxes. If the interior of the box is to be stained or lined with silk or skiver, this should be done first.

Fig. 70 shows a rectangular box with a deep lid, which is suitable for holding cigarettes, cards, trinkets or other articles. Cut two paper patterns, one to cover the back, top, and front of the box, and another pattern for the two identical pieces of leather that are to cover the two ends of the box. These pieces should be large enough to cover both the lid and the bottom part of each end. Cut out the three pieces of leather, and carry out the design by tooling, stamping or one of the other methods already described. Also, at this time, apply color of gold leaf, if desired.

Before applying the end pieces of leather, put the cover on the box and fasten it down tightly by means of rubber bands or string passed around the box from front to back. Cover the ends of the box with paste and let the paste dry for a few minutes, as the wood will absorb some of it. Then add more paste where there are any dry spots; but do not apply too much or it will spot the leather. Press the two leather end pieces in place, wiping off any excess paste with a cloth. Let the paste dry overnight or at least for several hours. Trim off any parts of the leather that may have stretched beyond the edges of the box. Then, with a razor blade, cut the leather along the line between the lid and the bottom part of the box, and remove the rubber bands or string fastened around the box.

Apply the third piece of leather in the same way, around the front, top, and back of the box, keeping the box closed and pressing the leather gently and smoothly in place. When this has been done, wrap a piece of cloth tightly around the box to keep the cover in place and also to prevent the wood from warping. After the paste has dried thoroughly, remove the cloth and trim off any parts of the leather extending beyond the edges of the box. Then cut the leather with a razor blade along the lines between the lid and the bottom part of the box, in back and front.

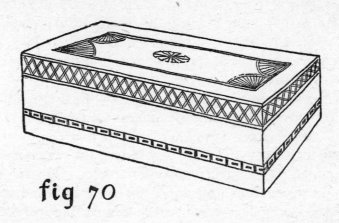

fig 70

Initials designed for Leatherwork.

BIBLIOGRAPHY

BIBLIOGRAPHY

ARTISTIC LEATHER CRAFT; Herbert Turner; *Sir I. Pitman & Sons, London and New York; 1926.*

DECORATION OF LEATHER; Georges de Récy; *London; 1905.*

DECORATIVE LEATHERWORK; Peter Wylie Davidson; *Longmans, Green & Co., New York; 1923.*

HANDICRAFT—SIMPLIFIED PROCEDURE AND PROJECTS; Lester Griswold; *Colorado Springs, Colorado; 1937.*

HIDES AND SKINS AND THE MANUFACTURE OF LEATHER; Paul Warburg; *The First National Bank, Boston; 1921.*

LEATHERCRAFT; *Grafton & Knight Co., Worcester, Mass.; 1929.*

LEATHERCRAFT AS A HOBBY; Clifford Pyle; *Harper & Brothers, New York; 1940.*

LEATHERCRAFT FOR AMATEURS; Eleanore E. Bang; *The Beacon Press, Boston; 1935.*

LEATHERWORK; Ivy P. Roseaman; *Dryad Press; Leicester, England; 1939.*

MAKE IT OF LEATHER; J. G. Schnitzer; *Government Printing Office, Washington, D. C.; 1939.*

PRACTICAL LEATHERWORK; Frederick Richard Smith; *Sir I. Pitman & Sons, London and New York; 1929.*

THE ART AND CRAFT OF LEATHERWORK; Cecile Francis-Lewis; *Seeley, Service & Co., London; 1928.*

WORKING WITH LEATHER; Maurice H. Decker; *Webb Book Publishing Co., St. Paul, Minnesota; 1935.*